The
Monarch Book
of
Sins & Virtues

The Monarch Book of Sins & Virtues

Compiled & Edited
by
David Porter

Monarch Books

First published by Monarch Books 1999

ISBN 1 85424 331 4

Editorial office: Monarch Books,
Broadway House, The Broadway, Crowborough,
East Sussex TN6 1HQ.

British Library Cataloguing in Publication Data
A catalogue record for this book is available
from The British Library.

Designed and typeset by David Porter Text & Editorial

Jacket Design: Bookprint Creative Services Ltd

Book production for the Publishers by
Gazelle Creative Productions Ltd, Concorde House,
Grenville Place, Mill Hill, London NW7 3SA.

For Donald Drew,
teacher and friend.

Contents

Preface

This anthology collects together material from many years' reading, and I hope that you will make some discoveries of your own as you explore it. I have attempted to mix the well known and the out of the way, and also to provide some explanation of how the well-known lists of the seven deadly sins and the seven virtues came to be compiled.

I have plundered a wide range of books and writings of all kinds. In older texts, where there was a problem of meaning, I have sometimes done some silent modernisation; but where the sense is clear (if old fashioned) I have left archaic expressions unchanged. This seemed preferable to cluttering the pages with glossaries for the sake of the few older extracts included. In some instances I have supplied my own translations, and in a couple of cases, footnotes. Regretfully, some abridging has been necessary, even where the quotation is itself part of a longer work.

The sources of all my quotations are listed at the end of the book, and I have tried where possible to make the references usable with any edition.

I am grateful to the publishers acknowledged on p.190 who have given permission for copyright material to be included, and to several friends and acquaintances, particularly Peter Cousins, Nigel Forde, Iona Opie, Anne Pilling and John Bridger, who have contributed suggestions for items to be included. I would also like to thank the staff of Petersfield Reference Library for their frequent help, and the staff of Petersfield Bookshop and of Alton Second-hand Books, where many of my happiest discoveries have been made. And I am glad to acknowledge the influence of my father, Laurence Porter, who, aided and abetted by my honarary uncles Ernest Oulton Lee and Robert Sopwith, made me into a bookworm; of my mother, Perle Porter, who bequeathed me a very well-thumbed copy of her dictionary of quotations; and of my schoolmaster at Birkenhead School, C.K. Stevens Esq.

I'm sure that every reader will have his or her own list of choices that I have made which they would not have made, and vice versa. But disagreeing with the compiler is part of the pleasure of anthologies, and I hope that the following pages will contain some interesting surprises.

David Porter
Greatham, spring 1999

Part I
The Seven Deadly Sins

Introduction

The seven deadly, or 'capital', sins are today just a saying,
perhaps even a joke. It's not surprising, in an age when 'sin'
is a word not much used outside religious circles, that the
idea that seven particular sins might be in any sense fatal
has been consigned to the quotation books – or has
sometimes been hijacked to do secular duty. When, for
example, in George Bernard Shaw's *Major Barbara*, the
atheist industrialist Andrew Undershaft preaches a
different gospel to that of Major Barbara of the Salvation
Army, he uses the seven deadly sins merely as a useful
symbol:

> *Undershaft:* In your Salvation shelter I saw poverty,
> misery, cold and hunger. You gave them bread and
> treacle and dreams of heaven. I give from three pound
> ten a week to twelve thousand a year. They find their
> own dreams; but I look after the drainage.
> *Barbara:* And their souls?
> *Undershaft:* I save their souls just as I saved yours.
> Barbara: You saved my soul! What do you mean?
> *Undershaft:* I fed you and clothed you and housed you.
> I took care that you should have money enough to live
> handsomely – more than enough; so that you could be
> wasteful, careless, generous. That saved your soul from
> the seven deadly sins ... Yes, the deadly seven. [*Counting
> on his fingers*] Food, clothing, firing, rent, taxes,
> respectability and children. Nothing can lift those seven
> millstones from Man's neck but money....[1]

For Shaw the seven deadly sins were a convenient
metaphor for his analysis of the social ills of the young
twentieth century, a neat way of using a phrase which
everybody knows to make a political point.

But it was very different in earlier more religious times, for the medieval person in the street struggling with the hard questions of faith. The world of the Middle Ages was one where death came often and usually came early, by sickness and the sword, by poverty and plague. In that world the seven deadly sins were very much a reality. Sin seemed to walk abroad just like men and women did. The biblical image contained in God's words to Cain – 'If thou doest not well, sin lieth at the door. And unto thee shall be his desire, and thou shalt rule over him'[2] – was a plausible and frightening one. When religious writers wrote about pride as a real person, was it not the same as the four dreadful horsemen who would bring war, famine and pestilence at the end of history?

Centuries earlier St Augustine talked to his sins by name, as a man speaking to his tormentors. In his autobiographical *Confessions*, he described how he was assailed by temptation in the weeks and months leading up to his conversion.

> It was, in fact, my old mistresses, trifles of trifles and vanities of vanities, who still enthralled me. They tugged at my fleshly garments and softly whispered: 'Are you going to part with us? And from that moment will we never be with you any more? And from that moment will not this and that be forbidden you for ever?'[3]

Where pagan societies imagined their gods as people who lived and feasted in a real Valhalla, an actual Mount Olympus, the very Halls of the Blest, medieval Christians had no difficulty with the idea that their vices and virtues might be regarded as living, breathing entities, to be feared and fought in a very practical way indeed. That is why so much early literature portrays them as real people of flesh and blood.

The first people to talk specifically about the seven

deadly sins were probably several groups of fourth-century monks who were known as the 'Desert Fathers' – the first Christian hermits. Turning their backs on the towns and cities of Egypt, Palestine, Arabia and Persia, they retreated into the desert in search of salvation. For the purposes of this book we do not need to know very much about why they did so.[4] But in the desert those early hermits, far from indulging in a super-spiritual, mystical world-flight, grappled with very practical questions of relationships and how one was to live one's life. They began to classify sins, as a help to understanding them; and they began to identify the virtues that they desired to cultivate in themselves:

> We read of Abbot Ammonas, who spent fourteen years praying to overcome anger, or rather, more significantly, to be delivered from it. We read of Abbot Serapion, who sold his last book, a copy of the Gospels, and gave the money to the poor, thus selling 'the very words which told him to sell all and give to the poor'. Another Abbot severely rebuked some monks who had caused a group of robbers to be thrown in jail, and as a result the shamefaced hermits broke into the jail by night to release the prisoners. Time and again we read of Abbots who refuse to join in a communal reproof of this or that delinquent, like Abbot Moses, that great gentle Negro, who walked into the severe assembly with a basket of sand, letting the sand run out through many holes. 'My own sins are running out like this sand,' he said, 'and yet I am come to judge the sins of another.'[5]

Whether or not the concept of the seven deadly sins appeared first in the discussions of the Egyptian Desert Fathers isn't known for certain. But their writings were very influential, and in their works and in those of others, the organisation of chief sins into a list of seven became a commonplace of Church life and teaching. The scheme demonstrated the way that sins relate to other sins, and provided a helpful way of analysing conduct and prescribing religious duties.

By the Middle Ages any citizen in Christendom could have recited the list. The seven deadly sins were well known not only because they were taught from the pulpit, but also because they had entered everyday speech. They appeared in popular writing as well as learned treatises, and as time went by they began to appear in 'literature' as the gap between folk culture and 'high art' slowly widened.

In 1606, for example, the playwright and pamphleteer Thomas Dekker published *The Seven Deadly Sins of London*, a lively and contemporary account of the great city that has been very useful to later historians. It is both a celebration of London life and a denunciation of it; Dekker, writing three years after a plague that killed 2,798 people in one week in the city, has an almost medieval sense of the judgement of God on the wicked city that he loves:

> O London, thou art great in glory, and envied for thy greatness: thy Towers, thy Temples, and thy pinnacles stand upon thy head like borders of fine gold, thy waters like fringes of water hang at the hems of thy garment. Thou art the goodliest of thy neighbours, but the proudest; the wealthiest, but the most wanton. Thou hast all things in thee to make thee fairest, and all things in thee to make thee foulest; for thou art attir'd like a bride, drawing all that look upon thee, to be in love with thee, but there is much harlot in thine eyes. Thou sits in thy Gates heated with wines, and in thy Chambers with lust.[6]

Geoffrey Chaucer (c. 1343-1400)

The seven deadly sins, however, had already appeared in a much more significant work of literature than any written by Thomas Dekker; in the work, in fact, that established

English, as distinct from Latin and French, as a language for writing literature in.

Geoffrey Chaucer's *Canterbury Tales* tells the story of a group of Canterbury pilgrims persuaded by their leader to while away the long journey by each in turn telling a story. The book draws heavily on medieval sources and on medieval theology. One of the pilgrims, a parson, gives us (as all the pilgrims do) a fascinating glimpse into fifteenth-century English life and times. He also reveals quite a lot about what the Church taught. The Parson is the last of the pilgrims to be called upon to tell a tale as the party nears Canterbury. But he insists that he has no intention of merely narrating an entertaining fable. He is going to preach them a sermon, a 'meditation' that will do them some good.

In the course of this 'Meditation', Chaucer, speaking through the Parson, embarks on a discussion of the seven deadly sins. (Chaucer got his information from a number of French medieval theological treatises.) Here is Chaucer's Parson on the sin of pride:

> Concerning Pride: though nobody can comprehensively tell you all the subdivisions of Pride and the many harms that come from it, I will show you a few of them. There are Disobedience, Vaunting Yourself, Hypocrisy, Despite, Arrogance, Impudence, Swollen-heart, Insolence, Conceit, Impatience, Strife, Contempt, Presumption, Irreverence, Pertinacity, Vainglory, and many other subdivisions that time does not permit me to explain. By disobedience I mean the man who holds God's commandments in contempt, who ignores what his rulers, or his spiritual father, tell him to do. By Vaunting Yourself I mean bragging about the bad things or the good things you have done. A hypocrite is somebody who conceals his true nature. A Despiteful person despises his neighbour – that is, his fellow Christian – or

he despises doing his duty. An arrogant man thinks that he is generous when in fact he is not; or he thinks that he deserves all he has; or he believes himself to be what he is not. Impudence means having no sense of shame about your sins. Swollen-heart means taking pleasure in the bad things you have done. Somebody is insolent when everybody else fails to measure up to his lofty standards of personal worth, of education, of accent and of deportment. Conceit means not deigning to acknowledge master or equal ...[7]

Chaucer (or his Parson) is now in full flight, summarising medieval thought beautifully, and many of the other pilgrims must have been wishing that somebody more entertaining had been chosen to round off the epic pilgrimage.

Another writer who tackled the subject of the seven deadly sins is William Langland, a fourteenth-century clergyman about whom very little is known. *Piers the Ploughman* tells the story of man's search for truth, and is seasoned with wit and observation. It also contains some of the most moving passages in medieval English religious verse, including the 'Harrowing of Hell', exploring the belief that during the three days of his burial Christ visited hell and led out the souls of godly believers of Old Testament times. At several points in the book Langland introduces the seven deadly sins as characters in his tapestry of English life.

Each of the sections that follow in the present book is introduced with a quotation from Langland, taken from the section of *Piers the Ploughman* that describes the seven deadly sins on their way to confession.

Pride

Dame Pernel Proud-of-Heart prostrated herself and lay for a long time stretched out on the ground. Then looking up she cried, 'Lord, have mercy on me'. She promised God that she would rip her shirt apart, and wear in its place a hair-shirt to subdue her flesh, so fiercely determined as it was to sin. 'Never now will I be taken by pride. Instead I will carry myself humbly. I'll put up with it when I am spoken of wrongly – and that's something I never did before! I am going to become meek, and plead for mercy. And that is something that I have always hated to do, deep in my heart.' [8]

Pride may seem a strange sin to place first out of seven. It's a failing that often seems ludicrous to those who observe it, either because it so easily turns into pomposity or because most proud claims seem unconvincing to lookers-on.

Yet pride can have very serious consequences. A good example is the old fable of the tailor who slew seven flies with his sword and proudly wore the inscription 'Slayer of Seven' ever afterwards – a proud boast that got him into a great deal of trouble later on. David, after his conquest of Goliath, was unfairly suspected of the same sin of pride by King Saul, with dreadful results:

When the men were returning home after David had killed the Philistine, the women came out from all the towns of Israel to meet King Saul with singing and dancing, with joyful songs and with tambourines and lutes. As they danced, they sang:
> 'Saul has slain his thousands,
> and David his tens of thousands.'
Saul was very angry; this refrain galled him. 'They have credited David with tens of thousands,' he thought, 'but

19

me with only thousands. What more can he get but the kingdom?' And from that time on Saul kept a jealous eye on David.[9]

In religion, pride is measured against the ultimate backdrop; the sheer impudence of finite, limited, ignorant humanity measuring itself against a supernatural God or gods: in the major religions a God who is infinite, omnipotent and omnipresent; in tribal and cultic religion, gods who are far more powerful than mankind.

In Islam, pride is the worst of all sins, because it is linked to ingratitude. Moslems reject the Judeo-Christian doctrine of original sin, and believe that Allah forgave Adam and exonerated him without the need for a redeemer. To be an unbeliever, to discount Allah's supreme forgiveness, is for Moslems the ultimate sinful pride because it is the ultimate ingratitude. That is why the Arabic word for an unbeliever is *kafir*, which means 'an ungrateful one'.

In Christianity, the sin of pride is even greater. Ignoring God means not only rejecting his generosity but also his sacrifice of himself, when – in the person of Jesus Christ, his Son – he was crucified. This gratuitous act of free grace lies behind many of the Bible's comments on pride.

Dante Alighieri (1265-1321)

Dante's epic trilogy *The Divine Comedy* stands as a summary of medieval theology and of medieval European culture itself. It describes the visionary spiritual travels of Dante during Easter 1300, and the revelations of divine truth given him by his idealised and adored symbol of romantic love, Beatrice.

Dante's travels take him through hell, purgatory and heaven, in a journey that is closely mapped according to medieval cosmology; so the seven deadly sins and the seven virtues are prominent. Here is Dante's soliloquy as he observes the souls of those who were proud in life, now suffering in purgatory:

> O ye proud Christians, wretched and weary, who, sick in mental vision, put trust in backward steps, perceive ye not that we are worms, born to form the angelic butterfly that flieth to judgement without defence? Why doth your mind soar on high, since ye are as 'twere imperfect insects, even as the grub in which full form is wanting?[10]

W. E. Henley (1849-1903)

So the confident assurance of W. E. Henley's famous anthem 'Invictus' can be regarded, depending on your point of view, as heroic fortitude or what the ancient Greeks called *hubris* – the dangerous state of mind that often accompanies success.

> Out of the night that covers me
> Black as the pit from pole to pole,
> I thank whatever gods may be
> For my unconquerable soul.
>
> In the fell clutch of circumstance
> I have not winced or cried aloud:
> Under the bludgeonings of chance
> My head is bloody, but unbow'd.
>
> Beyond this place of wrath and tears
> Looms but the Horror of the shade,
> And yet the menace of the years
> Finds and shall find me unafraid.
>
> It matters not how strait the gate,
> How charged with punishments the scroll,
> I am the master of my fate:
> I am the captain of my soul.

A more modern version of the same, echoing Henley's creed, is a song that was written by Paul Anka but will be for ever associated with Frank Sinatra, one of the great masters of twentieth-century popular song. Its title and refrain added an unforgettable phrase to the English language: 'I did it my way.'

Richard Wagner (1813-1883)

The distinction between heroic belief in one's own self-worth, and pompous arrogance, is often a small one. In December 1861 the composer Richard Wagner, impoverished by several business failures, wrote to a certain Baron von Hornstein peremptorily demanding a loan of 10,000 francs and three months hospitality at 'one of your estates, preferably in the Rhine district'. The Baron's reply, especially in view of Wagner's abuse of von Hornstein's friendship in the past and the arrogant tone of the composer's letter, was commendably meek. He regretted that he was unable to help; Wagner had over-estimated the von Hornstein wealth and lifestyle, and should seek wealthier patrons who were 'really rich'; nor was a three-month visit possible at that time, though it might be later. He concluded by expressing his wish that Wagner's opera *Tristan and Isolde*, of which a production had just been cancelled, would yet be heard. This conciliatory letter provoked Wagner to new, near-apoplectic heights of arrogance.

Paris, 27th December, 1861

DEAR HERR VON HORNSTEIN – It would be wrong of me to pass over without censure an answer such as you have given me. Though it will probably not happen again that a man like me will apply to you, yet a perception of the impropriety of your letter ought of itself to be a good thing for you.

You should not have presumed to advise me in any way, even as to who is really rich; and you should have left it to myself to decide why I do not apply to the patrons and patronesses to whom you refer.

If you are not prepared to have me at one of your estates, you could have seized the signal opportunity I offered you of making the necessary arrangements for receiving me in some place of my choice. It is consequently offensive of you to say that you will let me know when you will be prepared to have me.

You should have omitted the wish you express with regard to my *Tristan*; your answer could only pass muster on the assumption that you are totally ignorant of my works.

Let this end the matter. I reckon on your discretion, as you can on mine – Yours obediently.

Richard Wagner.[11]

George Bernard Shaw (1856-1950)

Many anecdotes are told of Shaw's conceit; many are certainly apocryphal and some, which do not quote him accurately, are unfair. Which leaves quite a few more!

The distinguished French writer Anatole France recollected the words with which Shaw introduced himself on their first meeting:

'Me too – I'm a genius too.'

Anatole France took it as a great compliment.[12]

James Boswell (1740-1795)

It seems that distinguished Frenchmen bring out the worst in arrogant British writers. Boswell was the companion and biographer of the English writer Dr Samuel Johnson. While still a young man, he met the celebrated author and philosopher Jean-Jacques Rousseau. The great Frenchman, who appears to have been a little at a loss as to what to make of his exuberant Scottish visitor, bade him farewell with a well-turned flattery:

'Adieu! You are a gentleman!'

Boswell agreed. 'You have shown me great kindness! – I deserve it!'[13]

Oscar Wilde (1854-1900)

No French prompters for Oscar Wilde, whose published maxims include, 'To love oneself is the beginning of a life-long romance.'[14] But he did astonish the Americans when he arrived in New York in 1882 to begin a lecture tour, having been preceded by great notoriety and stories of his flamboyant aesthetic lifestyle in London:

> The reporters who mobbed him on the boat were a little downcast by his appearance, which was more like that of an athlete than an aesthete. True, he had long hair, and he wore a bottle-green fur-lined overcoat, with a round sealskin cap on his head, but he was a giant in literature and his fists looked formidable. He naturally expected them to question him concerning his mission; instead they asked him how he liked his eggs fried, what he slept in, how he trimmed his finger-nails, and what temperature he liked his bath to be ... Wilde realized that he had not done himself justice on the boat, so he made up for it the moment he stepped ashore. 'Have you anything to declare?' asked the customs official. 'No. I have nothing to declare.' He paused. 'Except my genius.' Few remarks in history have travelled as widely and quickly as that one.[15]

John Donne (1573-1632)

Oscar was nothing without an audience; he blossomed in public and needed other people as a foil for his jokes and an audience for his plays. Which is a characteristic of pride, as John Donne observed in a sermon of 1619.

Solitude is not the scene of Pride; the danger of Pride is in company, when we meet to look upon another. But in Adam's wife, Eve, her first act (that is noted) was an act of Pride, a hearkening to that voice of the Serpent, *Ye shall be as Gods.* As soon as there were two, there was pride. How many may we have known (If we have had any conversation in the world) that have been content all the week, at home alone, with their worky day faces, as well as with their worky day clothes, and yet when they come on Sundays, when they come to Church, and appear in company, will mend both, their faces as well as their clothes. Not solitude, but company is the scene of pride ...

So early, so primary a sin is Pride, as that it grew instantly from her, whom God intended for a *Helper,* because he saw *that it was not good for man to be alone.* God sees that it is not good for man to be without health, without wealth, without power, and jurisdiction, and magistracy, and we grow proud of our helpers, proud of our health and strength, proud of our wealth and riches, proud of our office and authority over others ...

And as our pride begins in our Cradle, it continues in our graves and Monuments ... And such as have given nothing at all to any pious uses, or have determined their alms and their dole which they have given, in that one day of their funeral, and no farther, have given large annuities, perpetuities, for new painting their tombs, and for new flags, and scutcheons, every certain number of years.

O the earliness! O the lateness! How early a Spring, and no Autumn! How fast a growth, and no declination, of this branch of this sin Pride, against which, this first word of ours, *Sequere – Follow* – is opposed! This love of place, and precedency, it rocks us in our Cradles, it lies down with us in our graves. [16]

Kenneth Grahame (1859-1932)

But if we are speaking of pride as conceit, few fictional characters illustrate that sin better than Kenneth Grahame's Toad in *The Wind in the Willows* (who, it has been suggested, was modelled partly on Wilde[17]). Here is one of his poetic self-portraits: 'It was,' comments Grahame, 'perhaps the most conceited song that an animal ever composed … There was a great deal of the same sort, but too dreadfully conceited to be written down. These are some of the milder verses.'

> The world has held great Heroes,
> As history-books have showed;
> But never a name to go down to fame
> Compared with that of Toad!
>
> The clever men at Oxford
> Know all there is to be knowed
> But they none of them know
> one half as much
> As intelligent Mr Toad!
>
> The animals sat in the Ark and cried
> Their tears in torrents flowed.
> Who was it said, 'There's land ahead'?
> Encouraging Mr Toad!
>
> The army all saluted
> As they marched along the road.
> Was it the King? Or Kitchener?
> No. It was Mr Toad!
>
> The Queen and her Ladies-in-Waiting
> Sat at the window and sewed.
> She cried, 'Look! Who's that *handsome* man?'
> They answered 'Mr Toad!'[18]

Pride of this order does have its engaging side, and when we read *The Wind in the Willows* we never feel quite so outraged at Toad's vanity as do the other characters.

Some arrogant anecdotes to end this section, then, that leave one chuckling rather than condemning.

A little girl went to a friend's birthday party and returned with a look of quiet satisfaction. Asked by her parents whether she had enjoyed herself, she told them triumphantly,

'I was the prettiest girl there!'

Her parents gently remonstrated with her. 'Maybe you should leave other people to decide that.'

'Oh, no,' she replied. 'I know I'm right. I could see all the other little girls.'

Legendary comedian Bob Hope, a keen golfer, is said to have once played an opponent who had left himself very well-placed to win the game on his next shot. Hope's only chance of winning was if his opponent missed – but the other player's ball was so close to the hole that victory seemed certain.

'Conceded?' suggested his opponent.

'You sure are,' said Hope.

His opponent doubled up with laughter. His stroke went wide and Hope won the match.

Very early in his career, Charlie Chaplin, who could see that he was fast becoming a bankable asset, told his employer, Mack Sennett, that he wanted a salary of one thousand dollars per week.

'But *I* don't make that!' said Sennett.

'I know it,' Chaplin replied firmly. 'But the public doesn't line up outside the box-office when your name appears as they do for mine.'

27

Wrath

Then Anger awoke, white-eyed and runny-nosed, his head hanging. 'I am Anger,' he said. 'I was a friar once, working as a gardener at the friary; my job was to graft shoots on to the stems. So I grafted falsehoods on to begging friars and on to preaching friars, until the lies I grafted produced leaves of lying, to flatter gentlefolk; then they blossomed abroad into ladies' bowers to hear confessions. And all that has borne fruit, for now people would rather go for absolution to these friars than to their own parsons!

Now that the parsons recognise that they're having to share the takings with the friars, these monied priests preach against them, and the friars tell them it's their own fault – as anybody will tell you! And when they preach to the people round here, I – Anger – go along with them and teach from *my* books!' [19]

Browning, Robert (1812-1889)

Is there some special quality about friary gardens that cultivates wrath? Or was the celebrated Victorian poet Browning – a master of poetic invective – perhaps familiar with Langland's poem, and might he have had it in mind when he wrote the following 'Soliloquy of the Spanish Cloister', the thoughts of a monk watching his despised fellow-monastic at work?

Rarely can one gardener have hated another so, though we never quite find out what it is about Brother Lawrence that prompted the hatred ... the poem is, with some regret, abridged for the present anthology.

> Gr-r-r – there go, my heart's abhorrence!
> Water your damned flower-pots, do!

28

If hate killed men, Brother Lawrence,
   God's blood, would not mine kill you?
What? Your myrtle-bush needs trimming?
   Oh, that rose has prior claims –
Needs its leaden vase filled brimming?
   Hell dry you up with its flames!
At the meal we sit together:
   Salve tibi! I must hear
Wise talk of the kind of weather,
   Sort of season, time of year:
Not a plenteous cork-crop: scarcely
   Dare we hope oak-galls, I doubt:
What's the Latin name for 'parsley'?
   What's the Greek name for Swine's Snout?

Whew! We'll have our platter burnished
   Laid with care on our own shelf!
With a fire-new spoon we're furnished,
   And a goblet for ourself,
Rinsed like something sacrificial
   Ere 'tis fit to touch our chaps –
Marked with L. for his initial!
   (He-he! There his lily snaps!) ...

There's a great text in Galatians,
   Once you trip on it, entails
Twenty-nine distinct damnations,
   One sure, if another fails:
If I trip him just a-dying,
   Sure of Heaven as sure can be,
Spin him round and send him flying
   Off to Hell, a Manichee?

Or, my scrofulous French novel
   On grey paper with blunt type!

29

Simply glance at it, you grovel
    Hand and foot in Belial's gripe:

If I double down its pages
    At the woeful sixteenth print,
When he gathers his greengages,
    Ope a sieve and slip it in't?

Or, there's Satan! – one might venture
    Pledge one's soul to him, yet leave
Such a flaw in the indenture
    As he'd miss till, past retrieve,
Blasted lay that rose-acacia
    We're so proud of! *Hy, Zy, Hine* ...
'St, there's Vespers! *Plena gratia*
    Ave, Virgo!' Gr-r-r – you swine![20]

The monk's wrath is excessive and hypocritical. The most 'damnations' to be found in any verse in Galatians appear in chapter 5 verses 19-21, where there are seventeen at most. The curse in the last stanza is probably drawn from witchcraft. The oaths the monk uses reflect Browning's own extreme anti-Catholicism, and the thought that his enemy might be tricked into hell for being a Manichaen heretic is doubly ironic as the angry monk (as theologically knowledgeable readers would have enjoyed spotting) himself displays more than a touch of Manichaeism. A clear case of 'Physician, heal thyself' – or in this case, 'Gardener, prune thyself'. There is much sharply observed comedy in Browning's merciless portrait.

    Human wrath, in fact, has a habit of looking very silly (has anybody ever worked out a way of stamping one's foot angrily while retaining one's dignity?), especially when there is a large element of bluster involved.

Lewis Carroll
(The Rev. Charles Lutwidge Dodgson, 1832-1898)

Here, two immortal characters squabble their way into English literature.

'Do you think it's going to rain?'

Tweedledum spread a large umbrella over himself and his brother, and looked up into it. 'No, I don't think it is,' he said: 'at least – not under *here*. Nohow.'

'But it may rain *outside?*'

'It may – if it chooses,' said Tweedledee: 'we've no objection. Contrariwise.'

'Selfish things!' thought Alice, and she was just going to say 'Good-night' and leave them, when Tweedledum sprang out from under the umbrella, and seized her by the wrist.

'Do you see *that?*' he said, in a voice choking with passion, and his eyes grew large and yellow all in a moment, as he pointed with a trembling finger at a small white thing lying under the tree.

'It's only a rattle,' Alice said, after a careful examination of the little white thing. 'Not a rattle-*snake*, you know,' she added hastily, thinking that he was frightened: 'only an old rattle – quite old and broken.'

'I knew it was!' cried Tweedledum, beginning to stamp about wildly and tear his hair. 'It's spoilt, of course!' Here he looked at Tweedledee, who immediately sat down on the ground, and tried to hide himself under the umbrella.

Alice laid her hand upon his arm and said, in a soothing tone, 'You needn't be so angry about an old rattle.'

'But it *isn't* old!' Tweedledum cried, in a greater fury than ever. 'It's *new*, I tell you – I bought it yesterday – my nice new RATTLE!' and his voice rose to a perfect scream.

All this time Tweedledee was trying his best to fold up the umbrella, with himself in it ...

'Of course you agree to have a battle?' Tweedledum said in a calmer tone.

'I suppose so,' the other sulkily replied, as he crawled out of the umbrella.[21]

Jonathan Swift (1667-1745)

A burning anger of a more serious, moral kind drives the satirist Swift. Swift's anger was righteous moral indignation, and as such reflects something of the wrath of God; whose wrath, because he needs nothing and therefore has no need to throw a tantrum, is never self-seeking and never looks pompous. It is an anger that is more of a virtue than a sin. It is the kind of anger that St Paul writes about and does not forbid: '"In your anger do not sin": Do not let the sun go down while you are still angry.'[22]

Swift is most famously angry in *Gulliver's Travels* (1727), in which disgust at humanity's crimes and follies finds a burning focus. But his anger was directed not at humanity, but at the irrationality lying at the heart of a fallen world:

> I do not hate mankind ... It is [you] who hate them, because you would have them reasonable animals, and are angry for being disappointed.[23]

One of Swift's most sustained exercises in wrath is the tract *A Modest Proposal for Preventing The Children of Poor People from being a Burthen to their Parents, or the Country, and for making them Beneficial to the Public* (1729). Swift with glacial, ironic anger proposes a solution to the extreme poverty and social deprivation of his native Ireland; that the children of the poor should be marketed as butcher's meat:

I am assured by our merchants, that a boy or girl, before twelve years old, is no saleable commodity, and even when they come to this age, they will not yield above three pounds, or three pounds and half a crown at most on the Exchange, which cannot turn to account either to the parents or the kingdom, the charge of nutriment and rags having been at least four times that value ... I do therefore humbly offer it to public consideration, that of the hundred and twenty thousand children [of the poor] twenty thousand may be reserved for breed, whereof only one fourth part to be males ... that the remaining hundred thousand may at a year old be offered in sale to persons of quality, and fortune, throughout the kingdom ... A child will make two dishes at an entertainment for friends, and when the family dines alone, the fore or hind quarter will make a reasonable dish, and seasoned with a little pepper or salt will be very good boiled on the fourth day, especially in winter ... I grant this food will be somewhat dear, and therefore very proper for landlords, who, as they have already devoured most of the parents, seem to have the best title to the children.[24]

Dr Samuel Johnson (1709-1784)

The trouble with anger expressed as satire is that unsubtle recipients do not always get the point.

When Philip Stanhope, Earl of Chesterfield, somewhat belatedly began to recognise Johnson's genius and to use his influence to promote the great writer – at a time when Johnson had by now secured his own reputation by his own efforts – Johnson wrote him a letter that has become a classic of scorn, subtle invective and crushing irony.

To be so distinguished is an honour which, being very little accustomed to favours from the Great, I know not well how to receive, or in what terms to acknowledge ...

Seven years, My lord, have now past since I waited in your outward Rooms or was repulsed from your Door, during which time I have been pushing on my work through difficulties of which it is useless to complain, and have brought it at last to the verge of Publication without one Act of assistance, one word of encouragement, or one smile of favour. Such treatment I did not expect, for I never had a patron before....

Is not a Patron, My lord, one who looks with unconcern on a Man struggling for Life in the Water and when he has reached ground encumbers him with help? The notice which you have been pleased to take of my Labours, had it been easy, had been kind; but it has been delayed until I am indifferent and cannot enjoy it, till I am solitary and cannot impart it, till I am known and do not want it ...

I hope it is no very cynical asperity not to confess obligation where no benefit has been received, or to be unwilling that the Public should consider me as owing that to a Patron, which Providence has enabled me to do for myself.

Having carried my work thus far with so little obligation to any Favourer of Learning I shall not be disappointed though I should conclude it, if less be possible, with less, for I have been long wakened from that Dream of hope, in which I once boasted myself with so much exaltation,

My lord,
Your Lordship's Most humble
Most Obedient Servant
S. J.[25]

The noble Earl, who was fast becoming a connoisseur of literature – even if too late for Dr Johnson – was delighted with the letter. He considered it a masterpiece of prose, and showed it to all his visitors with the greatest pride.

G.K. Chesterton (1874-1936)

The speech by F.E. Smith (later Lord Birkenhead), in which he opposed the Parliamentary Bill for the Disestablishment of the Welsh Church, roused the ire of G.K. Chesterton in several ways. First, as a prosecuting barrister at the Old Bailey, Smith had humiliated Chesterton's brother Cecil in court through a ruinous libel action against him; the case had outraged G.K. Chesterton. Secondly, Smith's speech was pompous and wordy, and Chesterton took particular exception to the statement that Welsh Disestablishment would shock the conscience of every Christian community in Europe. This was clearly piffle. Chesterton took up his pen, dipped it in vitriol, and wrote 'Antichrist: Or, The Reunion of Christendom: An Ode.'

The following stanzas show the flavour of this accomplished and furious wrath, a tirade of rare poetic invective:

> Are they clinging to their crosses,
> F.E. Smith?
> Where the Breton boat-fleet tosses,
> Are they, Smith?
> Do they, fasting, trembling, bleeding,
> Wait the news from this our city?
> Groaning 'That's the Second Reading!'
> Hissing 'There is still Committee!'
> If the voice of Cecil falters,
> If McKenna's point has pith,
> Do they tremble for their altars?
> Do they, Smith? ...

35

In the lands where Christians were,
   F.E. Smith,
In the little lands laid bare,
   Smith, O Smith!
Where the Turkish bands are busy,
 And the Tory name is blessed
Since they hailed the cross of Dizzy
 On the banners of the West!
Men don't think it half so hard if
 Islam burns their kin and kith,
Since a curate lives in Cardiff
   Saved by Smith.

It would greatly, I must own,
   Soothe me, Smith!
If you left this theme alone,
   Holy Smith!
For your legal cause or civil
 You fight well and get your fee;
For your God or dream or devil
 You will answer, not to me.
Talk about the pews and steeples
 And the Cash that goes therewith!
But the souls of Christian peoples ...
   Chuck it, Smith![26]

Why does anger so often go wrong, and what started out as righteous indignation become petty, vindictive or self-seeking? Anger is always perilously close to sin, as the Bible warns: 'In your anger do not sin; when you are on your beds, search your hearts and be silent,' warns the Psalmist, and St Paul quotes the warning centuries later: '"In your anger do not sin": Do not let the sun go down while you are still angry.'[27]

The trouble usually starts when the angry person puts him or herself into the role of moral guardian, and plots revenge, or despises the hated person. It is the opposite of forgiveness. Angry people, in this sense, are no longer able to forgive. Thus anger can easily turn to hatred, and the angry person becomes judge, executioner, and ultimately tries to be God.

Larry Crabb (b. 1944)

Anger and its management is one of the major pre-occupations of psychiatry (and of medicine, for it is well-established that anger is the cause of many diseases, from minor ailments to terminal conditions). Here is the American psychologist and counsellor Larry Crabb, describing a trip by car to the pizza restaurant:

> I approached Second Avenue, driving East on Glades Road. The restaurant was located a mile north on Second Avenue, requiring that I turn left from Glades. I therefore eased the car into the left-hand lane, stopped because the light was red, and pressed the left-hand turn signal.
>
> After a few moments of waiting, the light turned green. Before I had a chance to put my plan into action, my wife said, 'Take a left here, honey.'
>
> Five simple words – *take a left here honey* – and I felt furious. I jerked my head toward her, snapped, 'I know', and stepped on the gas. Everything in me wanted to turn right but my desire for pizza outweighed my desire for revenge, so I turned left. Words flooded my mind, begging for release through my mouth, expressions of something other than appreciation for her help. Because the other people in the car were seeing me for counselling, I chose not to share those words with my wife.
>
> I felt angry, far more so than my wife's lack of confidence in my navigational skills seemed to justify.

I could have honestly stated that I was deeply committed to my wife, but at that moment the commitment was barren of emotional warmth.

Under my capable direction, we drove down Second Avenue until we saw the huge, well-lit sign that announced 'Pizza'. Just as I prepared to turn, my wife pointed and said, 'Here it is!' My rage doubled. Why? Certainly a host of questions, some a bit threatening, emerges from this rather ordinary incident:

• What does the intensity of my anger say about my level of maturity?

• Was my wife really not sure I knew where I was going, or was she acting out of casual habit and a real desire to be helpful?

• How should a husband best handle angry emotions toward his wife? Discuss it later? Label himself too sensitive and forget it? Get things into perspective by rehearsing her good points? Spew out his feelings in the name of honesty? Repent of his anger and ask God's help to be warm?[28]

Jonathan Edwards (1703-1758)

Larry Crabb suggests that anger might be an indicator of maturity – a point that is also made by Jonathan Edwards, the greatest theologian and philosopher of American Puritanism:

The passion of *anger*, in particular, seems to have been unluckily chosen as a medium to prove a sense and determination to delight in virtue, consisting in benevolence natural to all mankind. For if that moral sense which is exercised in anger, were that which arose from a benevolent temper of heart, being no other than a sense or relish of the beauty of benevolence, one would think, a disposition to anger should *increase*, at least in some proportion, as a man had more of a sweet, benign and benevolent temper; which seems contrary to experience, which shows that the less men have of benevolence, and the more they have of a contrary temper, the more are they disposed to anger and deep resentment of injuries.

And though *gratitude* be that which many speak of as a certain noble principle of virtue, which God has implanted in the hearts of all mankind; and though it be true there is a gratitude that is *truly virtuous*; and the want of gratitude, or an ungrateful temper, is *truly vicious*, and argues an abominable depravity of heart; yet I think, what has been observed may serve to convince such as impartially consider it, not only that all anger, or hating those which hate us, but also that not all gratitude, or loving those which hate us, arises from a truly benevolent heart.[29]

If righteous anger is such a wonderful thing, why are not mature people angry more often?

Because, Edwards reminds us, most anger is not righteous at all.

And anger of the other kind is at best ludicrous and at worst destructive, whether it spoils an evening at a pizza restaurant or brings about a world war.

Worthy to be called a sin, and a deadly one at that....

William Blake (1757-1827)

Blake, who was an uncomfortably unorthodox poet, had some commonsense words to say about anger:

> I was angry with my friend;
> I told my wrath, my wrath did end.
> I was angry with my foe:
> I told it not, my wrath did grow.[30]

The theme that anger bottled up is a source of sickness and bitterness is a typical Blake theme. But it's a complex matter, for the wrath of God is also part of the equation:

> A robin red breast in a cage
> Puts all Heaven in a rage.[31]

The characteristic simplicity of Blake's writing masks the ambivalence of anger that he portrays. 'Damn braces: Bless relaxes', he observed[32], but also remarked that: 'The tygers of wrath are wiser than the horses of instruction.'[33]

The reason for the ambivalence is that Blake's attitude to the seven deadly sins was unorthodox in itself. He added to them the sin of shame, and believed that they were originally permitted and considered good. In 'Urizen' he describes how they became 'The Seven Deadly Sins of the Soul', and in 'The French Revolution' he gives a compelling description of their nature.

> In the den nam'd Religion, a loathsome sick
>   woman bound down
> To a bed of straw; the seven diseases of earth,
>   like birds of prey, stood on the couch
> And fed on the body ...[34]

Whatever their origins, the deadly sins have become, in Blake's eyes, truly terrible: carved on the Eastern gate of Golgonooza, looking towards Beulah (representing the subconscious mind), 'the seven diseases of the earth are carved terrible'.[35]

Blake recognises only one solution to this dreadful problem: the healer, Jesus.

> All Mental Powers by Diseases we bind,

But he heals the deaf & the Dumb
&. the Blind.
Whom God has afflicted for Secret Ends
He comforts & Heals & calls them Friends ...

There is not one Moral Virtue that Jesus Inculcated but Plato & Cicero did inculcate before him; what then did Christ inculcate? Forgiveness of Sins. This alone is the Gospel, & this is the Life & Immortality brought to light by Jesus.[36]

Blake is dangerous stuff, but then so too are deadly sins; and much of his notorious contempt for established Christianity was due to his perception that it had gone soft on sins and the necessity of forgiving them.

Wrathful words

A few wrathful one-liners before we move on:

Anger makes dull men witty, but it keeps them poor.
*Francis Bacon (1561-1626), sometimes
attributed to Elizabeth I.*

War hath no fury like a non-combatant.
C.E. Montague (1867-1928),
Disenchantment *(1922).*

I renounce war for its consequences, for the lies it lives on and propagates, for the undying hatred it arouses, for the dictatorships it puts in the place of democracy, for the starvation that stalks after it.
H.E. Fosdick (1874-1969), Armistice Day Sermon,
The Secret of Victorious Living *(1934).*

41

Bigotry may be roughly defined as the anger of men who have no opinions.

G.K. Chesterton (1874-1936),
Heretics (1905).

It's interesting to live when you are angry.

Yevgeny Yevtushenko (b. 1933)
quoted from The Observer *(1962) in*
The Penguin Book of Modern Quotations *(1971)*

Watts, Isaac (1674-1748)

The last word on wrath we leave to wise old Isaac Watts, ever keen to derive the last ounce of moral exhortation on the slightest pretext.

> Birds in their little nests agree;
>   And 'tis a shameful sight,
> When children of one family
>   Fall out, and chide, and fight.
>
> Hard names at first, and threatening words,
>   That are but noisy breath,
> May grow to clubs and naked swords
>   To murder and to death.[37]

Quaint and amusing at this distance – but horribly up to date when one reads the daily newspapers.

Envy

His body was all swollen with wrath; he bit his lips and wrung his hands, brooding how he would take his revenge in deed or words when the chance came; every word those lips spat out was like an adder's tongue. His livelihood came from accusation and confrontation, with back-biting, slander and bearing false witness; they were the only good manners he was capable of, wherever he might turn up ...

'When I go to church, and I kneel before the cross and pray for the pilgrims, palmers and everybody else, just as the priest instructs us to – then on my knees I beseech Christ to give grief to those who carried off my begging bowl and my torn sheet. And then I switch my gaze away from the altar and I notice that Elaine is wearing a new coat, and immediately I wish it were mine – I want the coat and the roll of cloth it was made out of too!

I exult over somebody's losses, but if he shows a profit I weep and wail. I consider that people have done wrong, when I have done far worse. And if anybody rebukes me for it, I hate him for evermore with deadly hatred. What I really want is for everybody to be my slave, for I am sorely grieved over every person who has more possessions than I have.' [38]

Envy is the ultimate self-image problem, because it is the result of comparing oneself to others and deciding that they are better off (or indeed better) than oneself. Aware of this threat to self-esteem, the envious person tries to belittle other people, as if by proving that somebody else is doing badly proves that you are doing well ... Theologically it is regarded as a very bad sin indeed, because it not only destroys relationships, it disparages the grace of God who distributes his gifts to humanity without discrimination.

The opposite of envy is therefore humility, the state of being contented with one's lot and glad for the good fortune of other people. Here is St Paul, giving an object lesson in humility:

St Paul

> I rejoice greatly in the Lord that at last you have renewed your concern for me. Indeed, you have been concerned, but you had no opportunity to show it. I am not saying this because I am in need, for I have learned to be content whatever the circumstances. I know what it is to be in need, and I know what it is to have plenty. I have learned the secret of being content in any and every situation, whether well fed or hungry, whether living in plenty or in want. I can do everything through him who gives me strength.[39]

The Parable of the Prodigal Son

The dividing line between jealousy and envy is narrow. There is a huge difference between Paul's contentment and lack of envy of others, and the fit of sulks thrown by the brother of the returning prodigal. On the one hand, he wants what his brother has been given, the fatted calf and the party – this is envy. On the other hand, he bitterly resents the fact that his father appears to have switched his affection, previously his by right as the dutiful son, to his wastrel brother who has done nothing to deserve it and everything to lose it – this is jealousy.

> Jesus continued: 'There was a man who had two sons. The younger one said to his father, "Father, give me my share of the estate." So he divided his property between them. Not long after that, the younger son got together all he had, set off for a distant country

and there squandered his wealth in wild living. After he had spent everything, there was a severe famine in that whole country, and he began to be in need. So he went and hired himself out to a citizen of that country, who sent him to his fields to feed pigs. He longed to fill his stomach with the pods that the pigs were eating, but no-one gave him anything. When he came to his senses, he said, "How many of my father's hired men have food to spare, and here I am starving to death! I will set out and go back to my father and say to him: Father, I have sinned against heaven and against you. I am no longer worthy to be called your son; make me like one of your hired men." So he got up and went to his father.

But while he was still a long way off, his father saw him and was filled with compassion for him; he ran to his son, threw his arms around him and kissed him. The son said to him, "Father, I have sinned against heaven and against you. I am no longer worthy to be called your son." But the father said to his servants, "Quick! Bring the best robe and put it on him. Put a ring on his finger and sandals on his feet. Bring the fattened calf and kill it. Let's have a feast and celebrate. For this son of mine was dead and is alive again; he was lost and is found." So they began to celebrate.

Meanwhile, the older son was in the field. When he came near the house, he heard music and dancing. So he called one of the servants and asked him what was going on. "Your brother has come," he replied, "and your father has killed the fattened calf because he has him back safe and sound."

The older brother became angry and refused to go in. So his father went out and pleaded with him. But he answered his father, "Look! All these years I've been slaving for you and never disobeyed your orders.

Yet you never gave me even a young goat so I could celebrate with my friends. But when this son of yours who has squandered your property with prostitutes comes home, you kill the fattened calf for him!"

"My son," the father said, "you are always with me, and everything I have is yours."' [40]

Enid Blyton (1879-1968)

Envy is very close to spite, and is one of the most childish of sins. The prolific children's writer Enid Blyton, who published over 400 books, was adept not only at creating envious spiteful child characters, but in bringing about a fair amount of spite in her readers too on occasion. The unfortunate Susie dogs the meetings of the Secret Seven Society, a children's adventure club of which her brother is a member. It has few rules but one is most important: Susie can't join. Many of the plots of Blyton's Secret Seven stories include much plotting about to how to keep Susie out – though to be fair, this tells you as much about the Secret Seven Society and its creator as about the admittedly obnoxious little girl who is so desperate to join.

'Well, we're having a Secret Seven meeting jolly soon,' [Peter] said to Susie, making up his mind very suddenly that they would. 'But you're not coming! And if you try any silly snooping, you'll be sorry. You don't belong to our society, and you never will.'

'I know your last password,' said Susie, skipping over the cracks in the paving-stones. 'Aha!'

'You don't,' said Peter, racking his brains to remember what it was. Goodness – it wouldn't do for *him* to forget it!

'I do. It's Jack Sprat!' said Susie, and Peter scowled at her. She was right. Jack Sprat was the last password they had chosen – a secret password – and here was

Susie shouting it out in the road. She saw his angry face and laughed.

'I'm right, aren't I? Yours is a silly society. I know your password, and so do all the girls in my class. I told them. So the next time you have a meeting we'll all be along, shout out the password, and you'll have to let us in.' ...

'You're always snooping about, Susie!' said Peter, angrily. 'I never knew such a girl. Why can't you leave us alone, and not keep trying to find out our passwords and what we're doing?'

'Well, why don't you let me belong?' demanded Susie. 'You let Janet belong, and Pam and Barbara.'

'Don't be silly. It's the Secret *Seven* – we can't have any more members, or we'd be eight,' said Peter. 'Anyway – we don't want you, Susie.'

'You're mean,' said Susie.[41]

William Shakespeare (1564-1616)

Susie's envy is entirely the result of desiring something that others have and she feels unfairly deprived of.

It is a sin that is deadly to relationships, but it is different to the sin of jealousy, which is not included in the traditional seven deadly sins. Jealousy is usually a three-way relationship; a person is jealous of somebody else because a third party has transferred their affections or their loyalty to them. Shakespeare coined a memorable phrase for jealousy, in *The Merchant of Venice* – he called it 'green-eyed jealousy'[42] – and the phrase reappears in his major treatise on jealousy, the play *Othello* –

> O! Beware, my lord, of jealousy;
> It is the green-eyed monster which doth mock
> The meat it feeds on.[43]

In *Othello*, we discover the remarkable ambiguity of jealousy; Iago is jealous of Othello, who has been promoted over his head in the army; so he resolves to make Othello jealous of Cassio, Othello's lieutenant and friend both of Othello and his wife Desdemona. The means of making Othello jealous is to cause him to suspect his wife of unfaithfulness with Cassio. Iago's plans tragically succeed as the jealousy-maddened Othello murders the devoted and impeccably faithful Desdemona.

Here is Iago, skilfully playing the role of the concerned friend troubled about Othello's mounting jealousy, while at the same time adroitly feeding it:

> *Othello:* Ha! Ha! False to me?
> *Iago:* Why, how now, general! No more of that.
> *Othello:* Avaunt! Be gone! Thou hast set me on
> the rack:
> I swear 'tis better to be much abused
> Than but to know't a little.
> *Iago:* How now, my lord!
> *Othello:* What sense had I of her stolen hours
> of lust?
> I saw't not, thought it not, it harm'd not me:
> I slept the next night well, was free and merry;
> I found not Cassio's kisses on her lips:
> He that is robb'd, not wanting what is stol'n,
> Let him not know't and he's not robbed at all.
> *Iago:* I am sorry to hear this.
> *Othello:* I had been happy, if the general camp,
> Pioners* and all, had tasted her sweet body,
> So I had nothing known. O, now for ever

* *Pioner (Pioneer):* the equivalent of engineers in the modern army. Because Pioners were soldiers whose tools were not weapons of war, a fighting soldier like Othello would consider it a degrading occupation, hence the reference here.

Farewell the tranquil mind! Farewell content!
Farewell the plumed troop and the bog wars
That make ambition virtue! O farewell,
Farewell the neighing steed and the shrill trump,
The spirit-stirring drum, the ear-piercing fife
The royal banner and all quality,
Pride, pomp and circumstances of glorious war!
And you, O you mortal engines, whose
    rude throats
The immortal Jove's dread clamours counterfeit,
Farewell! Othello's occupation's gone!
Iago: Is't possible, my lord? ...
Othello: By the world,
I think my wife be honest, and think she is not;
I think that thou art just, and think thou art not:
I'll have some proof ... Would I were satisfied!
Iago: I see, sir, you are eaten up with passion:
I do repent me that I put it to you ....[44]

Shakespeare's intriguing point is that Othello does not kill
Desdemona because he hates her; he kills her because he
loves her so much that he cannot bear to imagine her with
another; and neither can he imagine life without her, for
having murdered her he immediately kills himself.

Othello was written in 1604, the same year as *Measure for
Measure* (see p.144), when Shakespeare was drawing on
Christian concepts strongly in his work. So there may well
be a sub-text, in this tragedy of jealousy intermingled with
exclusive, total love, that makes Othello's story bear some
resonances with the biblical account of the love of God;
just as divine anger is purely virtuous, so is divine jealousy
towards his people: as in the following Old Testament
passages from the Pentateuch, or the Books of Moses.

The Books of Moses

And God spoke all these words: 'I am the LORD your God, who brought you out of Egypt, out of the land of slavery. You shall have no other gods before me. You shall not make for yourself an idol in the form of anything in heaven above or on the earth beneath or in the waters below. You shall not bow down to them or worship them; for I, the LORD your God, am a jealous God, punishing the children for the sin of the fathers to the third and fourth generation of those who hate me, but showing love to a thousand [generations] of those who love me and keep my commandments.' [45]

Is this the way you repay the LORD, O foolish and unwise people? .... For the LORD's portion is his people, Jacob his allotted inheritance. In a desert land he found him, in a barren and howling waste. He shielded him and cared for him; he guarded him as the apple of his eye, like an eagle that stirs up its nest and hovers over its young, that spreads its wings to catch them and carries them on its pinions. The LORD alone led him; no foreign god was with him. He made him ride on the heights of the land and fed him with the fruit of the fields. He nourished him with honey from the rock, and with oil from the flinty crag, with curds and milk from herd and flock and with fattened lambs and goats, with choice rams of Bashan and the finest grains of wheat. You drank the foaming blood of the grape. Jeshurun grew fat and kicked; filled with food, he became heavy and sleek. He abandoned the God who made him and rejected the Rock his Saviour. They made him jealous with their foreign gods and angered him with their detestable idols. They sacrificed to demons, which are not God – gods they had not known, gods that recently appeared, gods your fathers did not fear. You deserted the Rock, who fathered you; you forgot the God who gave you birth. The LORD saw this and rejected them because he was angered by his sons and daughters. 'I will hide my face from them,' he said, 'and see what their end will be; for they are a perverse generation, children who are unfaithful. They made me jealous by what is no god and angered me with their worthless idols. I will make them envious by those who are not a people; I will make them angry by a nation that has no understanding .... They are a nation without sense, there is no discernment in them. If only they were wise and would understand this and discern what their end will be!'[46]

Lust

Then 'Alas!' said Lecher, and cried out to Our Lady to bring about mercy for his sins between God and his soul. For this he promised that for the next seven years, he would drink only water each Saturday, just as the ducks do, and eat but one meal that day.[47]

C.S. Lewis (1898-1963)

Lewis's *Pilgrim's Regress* (1933) was his first religious book, written during a holiday fortnight in Ireland while researching allegory in fiction, and before his reputation had been established as one of the century's greatest Christian apologists. It tells of John, who is travelling away from the 'Beautiful Island' and must encounter many people and places before his meeting with Mother Kirk sets him back on the right track. The tale obviously owes much to John Bunyan's *Pilgrim's Progress*, but its intellectual approach and the inexperience of its author in writing to persuade others of the truth of Christianity make it one of Lewis's least-read books. But there are many striking passages, not least the episode of the brown girl, with its powerful demonstration that lust has consequences.

> After that John was always going to the wood. He did not always have his pleasure of her in the body, though it often ended that way: sometimes he would talk to her about himself, telling her lies about his courage and his cleverness. All that he told her she remembered, so that on other days she could tell it over to him again. Sometimes, even, he would go with her through the wood looking for the sea and the Island, but not often. Meanwhile the year went on and the leaves began to fall in the woods and the skies

were more often grey: until now, as I dreamed, John had slept in the wood, and he woke up in the wood. The sun was low and a blustering wind was stripping the leaves from the branches. The girl was still there and the appearance of her was hateful to John: and he saw that she knew this, and the more she knew it the more she stared at him, smiling. He looked round and saw how small the wood was after all – a beggarly strip of trees between the road and a field that he knew well. Nowhere in sight was there anything that he liked at all.

'I shall not come back here,' said John. 'What I wanted is not here. It wasn't you I wanted, you know.'

'Wasn't it?' said the brown girl. 'Then be off. But you must take your family with you.'

With that she put up her hands to her mouth and called. Instantly from behind every tree there slipped out a brown girl: each of them was just like herself: the little wood was full of them.

'What are these?'

'Our daughters,' said she. 'Did you not know you were a father? Did you think I was barren, you fool? And now, children,' she added, turning to the mob, 'go with your father.'

Suddenly John became very much afraid and leaped over the wall into the road. There he ran home as fast as he could.[48]

Bernardo Bertolucci (b. 1940)

Of course lust means forgetting all such practical matters, including any needs but your own and any consequences whatsoever. The person lusted after becomes at worst an object, at best an animal. Here, in a novelisation of Bertolucci's film *Last Tango in Paris*, a couple who have come together simply out of lust discard even their names:

'I don't want a name. I'm better off with a grunt or a groan. Do you want to know my name?'

He raised himself on his hands and knees. He formed his mouth into the shape of a snout, lifted his head and growled loudly. Then he began to grunt, deep in his throat – a primal sound that excited them both....

'It's so masculine, she said. 'Now listen to mine.'

She pulled him down next to her on the mattress, and held him tightly. She mewed, and asked, 'Do you like it?'

They laughed. He grunted again, and she answered. Together they filled the circular room with the strident courtship of beasts.[49]

T.H. White (1906-64)

The bleak tragedy of *Last Tango in Paris* is the only outcome that can reasonably be expected when people treat other people as objects. There's an immense difference between lust and even the destructive, adulterous but still human love between, for example, Lancelot and Guenever, as T.H. White makes clear in his fictional version of their first awkward meetings:

'That's no good,' he said, and he began to unwind her hopeful work with angry fingers. His eyebrows made a horrible scowl.

There was a moment in which everything stood still. Guenever stood, hurt in her heart. Lancelot, sensing her stillness, stood also. The hawk stopped bating and the leaves did not rustle.

The young man knew, in this moment, that he had hurt a real person, of his own age. He saw in her eyes that she thought he was hateful, and that he had surprised her badly. She had been giving kindness, and he had returned it with unkindness. But the main thing was that she was a real person. She was not a minx, not deceitful, not designing and heartless. She was pretty Jenny, who could think and feel.[50]

William Shakespeare (1564-1616)

These two poles of desire – desiring a person and desiring an object – are opposing tendencies in the portrait Shakespeare paints in his poem 'The Rape of Lucrece'; here is Tarquin in one of his better moments, deliberating on whether or not to proceed with his plan to rape his intended victim:

> What win I, if I gain the thing I seek?
> A dream, a breath, a froth of fleeting joy.
> Who buys a minute's mirth to wail a week?
> Or sells eternity to get a toy?
> For one sweet grape who will the vine destroy?
>> Or what fond beggar, but to touch the crown
>> Would with the sceptre straight be strucken down?

But his lust overcomes his reason:

> I have debated, even in my soul,
> What wrong, what shame, what sorrow
>   I shall breed;
> But nothing can affection's course control,
> Or stop the headlong fury of his speed.
> I know repentant tears ensue the deed,
>> Reproach, disdain and deadly enmity;
>> Yet strive I to embrace mine infamy.

But she hath lost a dearer thing than life,
And he hath won what he would lose again;
This forced league doth force a further strife;
This momentary joy breeds months of pain;
    This hot desire converts to cold disdain:
    Pure Chastity is rifled of her store,
        And Lust, the thief, far poorer than
        before.[51]

Once again the consequences, for individual and state, are catastrophic, and Tarquin has well born out the explicit warning Shakespeare writes in one of his sonnets:

The expense of spirit in a waste of shame
Is lust in action; and, till action, lust
Is perjur'd, murderous, bloody, full of blame,
Savage, extreme, rude, cruel, not to trust;
Enjoy'd no sooner but despised straight;
Past reason hunted; and no sooner had,
Past reason hated, as a swallowed bait,
On purpose laid to make the taker mad:
Mad in pursuit, and in possession so;
Had, having, and in quest to have, extreme;
A bliss in proof, and proved, a very woe;
Before, a joy proposed; behind, a dream.
    All this the world well knows; yet none
        knows well
    To shun the heaven that leads men to
        this hell.[52]

George Bernard Shaw (1856-1950)

If love becomes lust when it abandons unselfish generosity and serves only itself, marriage becomes simply a venue for lust. In Shaw's *Man and Superman* (1903), he puts these words – appropriately enough – into the mouth of Don Juan.

What is virtue but the Trade Unionism of the married? ... Marriage is the most licentious of institutions: that is the secret of its popularity. And a woman seeking a husband is the most unscrupulous of all the beasts of prey. The confusion of marriage with morality has done more to destroy the conscience of the human race than any other single error.[53]

The Book of Common Prayer

Against which might be put the words of the Anglican Church's Marriage vows, which express that mutual giving which makes lust impossible.

I take thee to my wedded wife/husband, to have and to hold from this day forward, for better for worse, for richer for poorer, in sickness and in health, to love and to cherish, till death us do part, according to God's holy ordinance; and thereto I plight thee my troth ...

With this ring I thee wed, with my body I thee worship, and with all my worldly goods I thee endow: in the Name of the Father, and of the Son, and of the Holy Ghost. Amen.[54]

Dorothy L. Sayers (1893-1957)

Many nations today have been described as being dominated by lust; and not only sexual lust, for some of the world's sex capitals are also among its financial capitals. Is the consequence for nations the same kind of depersonalisation and degrading to which lust in individuals leads? Dorothy L. Sayers suggests that this is so:

Men and women may turn to lust in sheer boredom and discontent, trying to find in it some stimulus which is not provided by the drab discomfort of their mental and physical surroundings. When that is the case, stern rebukes and restrictions are worse than useless. It is as though one were to endeavour to cure anaemia by bleeding; it only reduces further an already impoverished vitality. The mournful and medical aspect of twentieth-century pornography and promiscuity strongly suggests that we have reached one of these periods of spiritual depression, where people go to bed because they have nothing better to do. In other words, the 'regrettable moral laxity' of which respectable people complain may have its root cause not in Luxuria [Lust] at all, but in some other of the sins of society, and may automatically begin to cure itself when that root cause is removed.[55]

Gluttony

There was laughing, and glowering, and people shouting 'Don't hang on to the cup!' Deals were made, and every deal was sealed with a drink; so they sat there until evensong, occasionally bursting into song, by which time Glutton had downed a gallon and a gill of ale. His guts were beginning to rumble like two greedy sows ... He could neither walk nor stand without his stick, and when he did get up he walked like a minstrel's bitch, sometimes veering to the side, sometimes going backwards, like somebody setting lines to trap fowl. When he got close to the door his eyes dimmed over, he staggered to the threshold and finally fell flat on his face. Clement the cobbler grabbed him round the middle trying to help him up, and managed to lift him back on to his knees. But Glutton was a large man and a terrible one to lift. As he knelt there, Glutton vomited into Clement's lap – a mess that smelt so horrible that the hungriest dog in Hertfordshire would have refused to lap it up.[56]

Kenneth Grahame (1859-1932)

What's the difference between gluttony and a mere healthy appetite? Why, for example, in *The Wind in the Willows* (1908), does Rat's picnic make you want to applaud Rat for his well-filled hamper, but Toad's picnic merely confirms your first unfavourable impressions? Here is Rat's hospitality –

After a short interval [the Rat] reappeared staggering under a fat, wicker luncheon-basket.

'Shove that under your feet,' he observed to Mole, as he passed it down into the boat. Then he untied the painter and took the sculls again.

'What's inside it?' asked the Mole, wriggling with curiosity.

'There's cold chicken inside it,' replied the Rat briefly: 'coldtonguecoldhamcoldbeefpickledgherkinsa aladfrenchrollscresssandwichespottedmeatgingerbeer lemonadesodawater – '

'O stop, stop,' cried the Mole in ecstasies: 'This is too much!'

'Do you really think so?' inquired the Rat seriously. 'It's only what I always take on these little excursions; and the other animals are always telling me that I'm a mean beast and cut it *very* fine!'[57]

And here is Toad's rather different hospitality, as he shows off his new caravan –

'There you are!' cried the Toad, straddling and expanding himself. 'There's real life for you, embodied in that little cart. The open road, the dusty highway, the heath, the common, the hedgerows, the rolling downs! Camps, villages, towns, cities! Here to-day, up and off somewhere else tomorrow! Travel, change, interest, excitement! The whole world before you ... And mind, this is the finest cart of its sort that was ever built, without any exception. Come inside and look at the arrangements. Planned 'em all myself, I did!' ...

'All complete!' said the Toad triumphantly, pulling open a locker. 'You see – biscuits, potted lobster, sardines – everything you can possibly want. Soda-water here – baccy there – letter-paper, bacon, jam, cards and dominoes – you'll find,' he continued, as they descended the steps again, 'you'll find that nothing whatever has been forgotten, when we make our start this afternoon.' ...

> During luncheon – which was excellent, of course,
> as everything at Toad Hall always was – the Toad
> simply let himself go.[58]

The difference is that Rat's feast is shared gladly with a
visitor; Toad merely uses hospitality as a way of promoting
himself. And where Toad's food is merely listed along with
his other material possessions, Rat clearly enjoys food for its
own sake.

Robert Farrar Capon (b. 1925)

For Rat, food is a pleasure, not an obsession – a distinction
highlighted by American Episcopalian priest and cook
Father Robert Farrar Capon, in his 'culinary entertainment', *The Supper of the Lamb* (1969). Here he is address-
ing the problem of Harry, who is dieting: a practice that
Father Capon has long repudiated.

> I passed my plate for seconds and then thirds, and
> made a vow then and there to walk more, to split logs
> every day and, above all, to change my religion from
> the devilish cult of dieting to the godly discipline of
> fasting ... My vow therefore was beautifully simple. If
> I ate, I would eat without stint; and if I stinted, I
> would not eat at all.
>
> I offer it as a prescription for Harry. Let him fast
> until he is free to eat like a true son of Adam. Let him
> take but one meal a day (or even one every other day,
> if he is one of the chosen ones whose metabolism
> marks him for a special vocation); let him fast in good
> earnest; nothing but liquids – no nibbles, no snacks.
> But then let him take meals worthy of the name ... It
> is bread that strengthens man's heart; it is the valleys
> thick with grain that laugh and sing. It is only when
> Harry, by feast and fast, lays a firm grip on the fatness

of the earth, that he himself will return to sanity and substance.

To begin with, real eating will restore his sense of the festivity of being ... A man's daily meal ought to be an exultation over the smack of desirability which lies at the roots of creation. To break real bread is to break the loveless hold of hell upon the world, and by just that much, to set the secular free.

But second, he will, by his fasting, be delivered from the hopelessness of mere gourmandise. The secular, for all its goodness, does not defend itself very well against mindless and perpetual consumption. It cries out to be offered to abstinence as well as use; to be appreciated, not simply absorbed: Hunger remains the best sauce. Beyond that, though, it cries out to be lifted into a higher offering still. The real secret of fasting is not that it is a simple way to keep one's weight down, but that it is a mysterious way of lifting creation into the Supper of the Lamb. It is not a little excursion into fashionable shape, but a major entrance into the fasting, the agony, the passion by which the Incarnate Word restores all things to the goodness God finds in them. It is as much an act of prayer as prayer itself, and, in an affluent society, it may well be the most meaningful of all the practices of religion – the most likely point at which the salt can find its savor once again. Let Harry fast in earnest, therefore. One way or another – here or hereafter – it will give him back his feasts.[59]

Laurie Lee (1914-1997)

The same thought is expressed in an essay by the poet Laurie Lee, on the subject of 'Appetite'.

Fasting is an act of homage to the majesty of appetite. So I think we should arrange to give up our pleasures regularly – our food, our friends, our lovers – in order to preserve their intensity, and the moment of coming back to them. For this is the moment that renews and refreshes both oneself and the thing one loves.[60]

Frank Richards (1876-1961)

However, it was Frank Richards (his real name was Charles Hamilton) who created possibly the most celebrated glutton in literature. Richards first wrote about Billy Bunter of Greyfriars School in 1907, and lived to write scripts for the successful TV adaptations. The Greyfriars books are still popular today, despite the fact that they often offend several major creeds of the politically correct – a revised series appeared in the 1980s, bringing the style up to date and discreetly altering some of Richards' enthusiasms. Yet Richards never despised Bunter or encouraged his readers to do so. A typical portrait of 'the Fat Owl of the Remove' ends *Billy Bunter of Greyfriars School* (1947), as Bunter stuffs himself with sweets, surrounded by his admiring schoolmates and even the usually forbidding teacher, Quelch – Bunter, by a complicated series of miraculous accidents, having emerged triumphant at the end.

> Mr. Quelch walked in. He had a box – rather a large cardboard box – in his hand. To the general astonishment, he gave Bunter a kindly smile.
>
> 'Bunter, I have brought you this small gift, not as a reward, of course, for your courageous act this afternoon, but as a token of my good opinion.' ...
>
> 'I say, you fellows.' [Bunter's] voice was a little muffled. 'I say, these toffees are prime! I say, Quelch is no fool! He knows how to treat a fellow who saved his

no fool! He knows how to treat a fellow who saved his life! I say, these toffees are topping.'

'Ha, ha, ha!'

Evidently Quelch had guessed the kind of gift that Bunter would appreciate! Bunter gobbled and beamed.

'I say, you fellows, have some of these toffees! There's lots – and lots – and lots! I say, Quelch ain't such a beast – ooogh – grooogh –. He ain't such a beast as you fellows think –. Grooogh! Ooogh! Wooogh!' Bunter choked, and coughed, and recovered. 'Urrrggh! I say, they're ripping! Have some, you fellows.'

And the fellows chuckled and had some.

It was a happy and sticky Owl …[61]

Vitellius 'The Glutton' (AD 15-69)

One historical character at least is remembered as a glutton because that was his name. Vitellius, a Roman military leader in Germany, was in AD 69 declared emperor by his soldiers, a title he made official by invading Italy. But the new emperor did not reward the soldiers who had brought him success, and he bungled badly in his attempts to make his reign secure. Those who had first acknowledged him as emperor were the first to plot against him. By October opposition to Vitellius was overwhelming; Vespasian's troops conquered Rome and Vitellius, his own army destroyed, died a violent and disreputable death at the hands of the victors.

He was notorious for cruelty and gluttony, and he acquired the nickname of 'The Glutton'. To have earned that title in an age noted for Roman excesses might seem to indicate that Vitellius must have been a champion glutton indeed, though it's thought by some historians that Vitellius' enemies exaggerated both his cruelty and his gluttony. After all, there would not be much glory in having defeated one of the most incompetent and unpopular of all the Roman emperors.

St Ignatius of Loyola (1491-1556)

If gluttony is such a destructive sin, how can it be cured? In his *Spiritual Exercises*, Ignatius provided some highly practical advice on disciplined eating.

> The seventh Rule, which should be carried out above all the rest, makes sure that his whole mind is not taken up with the food he is eating. He should not be so carried away by his appetite that he eats his food very quickly. Let him be master of himself both in the way he eats and in the quantity he eats.
>
> The eighth Rule is laid down so that he may overcome his desire for overeating. After dinner or after supper, or at any other time when he does not feel hungry, he should decide how much food will be eaten at the next meal. He must do this every day and plan how much to eat rather than give in to his appetite or give in to temptation. He should eat less rather then more when he is tempted to indulge himself in overeating.[62]

Bishop Desmond Tutu (b. 1931)

Gluttony, however, is not limited to food. Insatiable consumption of all kinds is a hallmark of modern society, often leading to great social injustice. Bishop Desmond Tutu wrote the following during the days of apartheid in South Africa:

> I come from a beautiful land, richly endowed by God with wonderful resources, wide expanses, rolling mountains, singing birds, bright shining stars out of

blue skies, with radiant sunshine, golden sunshine. There is enough of the good things that come from God's bounty: there is enough for everyone, but apartheid has confirmed some in their selfishness, causing them to grasp greedily a disproportionate share, the lion's share, because of their power.[63]

North	South
$\frac{1}{4}$ of the world's population	$\frac{3}{4}$ of the world's population
$\frac{4}{5}$ of the world's income	$\frac{1}{5}$ of the world's income
People can expect to live for 70 years or more	People can expect to live for 50 years
Most people can expect secondary education	Only $\frac{1}{2}$ of the population will have the chance of any formal education
Most people can get enough to eat	$\frac{1}{3}$ of the people will not get enough to eat
Uses $\frac{7}{8}$ of world's annual products of resources like petrol and gas	Uses $\frac{1}{8}$ of world's annual products of resources like petrol and gas
Eats nearly $\frac{2}{3}$ of world's annual supply of grain	Eats $\frac{1}{3}$ of world's annual supply of grain
Eats $\frac{4}{5}$ of world's annual production of protein	Eats $\frac{1}{5}$ of world's annual production of protein.[64]

The South African situation is a micro-picture of the world situation. The table above (by Kathy Keay) shows exactly what Western gluttony costs the Third World, in terms of relative prosperity across the global north/south divide.

Put so plainly, the sin of gluttony is clear to see in global, structural terms. And with it comes the necessity for its corollary, which we shall be considering later as one of the seven virtues – justice.

It's not as if the gluttonous North even needs the huge quantities that it consumes.

> The world is so full of a number of things
> I'm sure we should all be as happy as kings ...[65]

as Robert Louis Stevenson remarked.

Aldous Huxley (1894-1963)

The West already produces more waste than it knows what to do with, but for Aldous Huxley the future was a Brave New World of obsolescence, where over-consumption is compulsory. Here is the voice of the 'sleep-teacher':

> In the nurseries, the Elementary Class Consciousness lesson was over, the voices were adapting future demand to future industrial supply. 'I do love flying,' they whispered, 'I do love flying, I do love having new clothes, I do love ...'
> 'But old clothes are beastly,' continued the untiring whisper. 'We always throw away old clothes. Ending is better than mending, ending is better than mending, ... ending is better ...'
> 'Every man, woman and child compelled to consume so much a year. In the interests of industry. The sole result ...'
> 'Ending is better than mending. The more stitches, the less riches; the more stitches ...'[66]

Vance Packard (b. 1914)

American sociologist Vance Packard gained a wide reputation as a consumer guru when he published *The Hidden Persuaders*, which was a study of the power of advertising; he wrote a number of other books, including *The Waste Makers*, in which he quoted the above passage from Aldous Huxley as introduction to a discussion of 'the throw-away spirit'.

> The voice of the television announcer – in 1960 – chanted, 'You use it once and throw it away … You use it once and throw it away.' This specific chant was used to promote the sale of a deodorant pad. And a steel company, in a television commercial, showed a pleased housewife dropping a metal can that had contained soft drinks into the waste basket. No fussing with returns!
>
> Residents of the United States were discarding, using up, destroying, and wasting products at a rate that offered considerable encouragement to those charged with achieving ever-higher levels of consumption for their products. A business writer for *Time* magazine related, as the sixties were about to begin: 'The force that gives the U.S. economy its pep is being generated more and more in the teeming aisles of the nation's stores … U.S. consumers no longer hold on to suits, coats, and dresses as if they were heirlooms …. Furniture, refrigerators, rugs – all once bought to last for years of life – are now replaced with register-tingling regularity.' [67]

Several world recessions, the growth of Green politics, and recycling initiatives on local, national and global levels have all failed to radically change the high consumerism and waste production of the wealthy North.

The Book of Amos

Is gluttony a deadly sin? Theologically, there is no doubt of it. The prophet Amos denounced all national gluttony and over-consumption, and his words stand as condemnation to gluttonous societies throughout history.

> Hear this word, O house of Israel, this lament I take up concerning you ... You trample on the poor and force him to give you grain. Therefore, though you have built stone mansions, you will not live in them; though you have planted lush vineyards, you will not drink their wine. For I know how many are your offences and how great your sins. You oppress the righteous and take bribes and you deprive the poor of justice in the courts. Therefore the prudent man keeps quiet in such times, for the times are evil. Seek good, not evil, that you may live. Then the LORD God Almighty will be with you, just as you say he is. Hate evil, love good; maintain justice in the courts. Perhaps the LORD God Almighty will have mercy on the remnant of Joseph....
>
> Woe to you who long for the day of the LORD! Why do you long for the day of the LORD? That day will be darkness, not light. It will be as though a man fled from a lion only to meet a bear, as though he entered his house and rested his hand on the wall only to have a snake bite him. Will not the day of the LORD be darkness, not light – pitch-dark, without a ray of brightness? I hate, I despise your religious feasts; I cannot stand your assemblies. Even though you bring me burnt offerings and grain offerings, I will not accept them. Though you bring choice fellowship offerings, I will have no regard for them. Away with the noise of your songs! I will not listen to the music of your harps. But let justice roll on like a river, righteousness like a never-failing stream!' [68]

Avarice

'I have been covetous,' the wretch said. 'I'm owning up to it, here and now. For a time I was in service as an apprentice to Sim-at-the-Stile, contracted to see him profitable. I started out with a mere page or two of lies, but my first lesson was how to weigh dishonestly. I attended the fairs at Weyhill and Winchester under my master's orders, carrying with me all sorts of merchandise. Had not the luck of guile found its way into my stock, my goods would have remained unsold these seven years – God is my witness!

Then I took myself off to educate myself among the drapers. They showed me how to pull out the selvages so that the rolls looked longer than they really were. I learned another lesson when I worked with the striped fabrics; how to sew them with pack-needles, fold them up, and put them in a press until ten or twelve yards stretched out to make thirteen ... But I swear now, as I hope to prosper, I'm going to abandon my deceptions and give no more short measure or use sharp practice.' [69]

Avarice is not the same as gluttony. A glutton is somebody who has an appetite that has got out of control, and consumes to excess. Somebody who is avaricious is somebody who is driven by an insatiable desire to possess, to accumulate. It is the sin that used to be called covetousness. It is the sin of wanting what is not yours, of wanting something for nothing, of gain without pain; and it characterises much of modern life.

A glutton will reach a point where his appetite will be satisfied, at least for a time; but for the avaricious person, avarice is inextricably part of their character, and getting what they want so badly is hardly ever so satisfying as wanting it was.

St Augustine (AD 354-430)

Augustine illustrates well the fact that the rewards of avarice frequently turn sour in the following account of his theft, as a teenager, of some pears. A variety of deadly sins play a part in this avaricious exploit. Augustine, as is his habit, speaks directly to his sin as if to a real person:

> What was it in you, O theft of mine, that I, poor wretch, doted on you – you deed of darkness – in that sixteenth year of my age? Beautiful you were not, for you were a theft. But are you anything at all, so that I could analyse the case with you? Those pears that we stole were fair to the sight because they were thy creation, O Beauty above compare, O Creator of all, O thou good God – God the highest good and my true good. Those pears were truly pleasant to the sight, but it was not for them that my miserable soul lusted, for I had an abundance of better pears. I stole those simply that I might steal, for, having stolen them, I threw them away. My sole gratification in them was my own sin, which I was pleased to enjoy; for, if any one of these pears entered my mouth, the only good flavour it had was my sin in eating it.
>
> And now, O Lord my God, I ask what it was in that theft of mine that caused me such delight; for behold it had no beauty of its own – certainly not the sort of beauty that exists in justice and wisdom, nor such as is in the mind, memory senses, and the animal life of man; nor yet the kind that is the glory and beauty of the stars in their courses; nor the beauty of the earth, or the sea – teeming with spawning life, replacing in birth that which dies and decays, Indeed, it did not

have that false and shadowy beauty which attends the deceptions of vice.[70]

Mark Twain
(Samuel Langhorne Clemens, 1835-1910)

The same idea was succinctly expressed, with characteristically mordant wit, by the American humorist Mark Twain:

> Adam was but human – this explains it all. He did not want the apple for the apple's sake, he wanted it because it was forbidden. The mistake was in not forbidding the serpent; then he would have eaten the serpent.[71]

George MacDonald (1824-1905)

Best known for a handful of fantasy novels and for having had a strong literary and spiritual influence on C.S. Lewis, MacDonald was the author of many books, not all of which match the standard of, for example, *Lilith*, *Fantastes*, and *At the Back of the North Wind*. *What's Mine's Mine* is one of his second-rank books, in which the desire to morally instruct his reader constrains his imaginative and literary qualities. The book contains, as its title suggests, much on selfishness, avarice and greed. It is based on a true story of a greedy landlord's exploitation and oppression, which had moved MacDonald deeply. In the following exchange, he sets out, like a schoolmaster, the bones of the issue.

> 'I have a fear, Alister, that you are in danger of avarice,' said Ian after a pause.
> 'Avarice, Ian! What can you mean?'
> 'You are as free, Alister, from the love of money, as any man I ever knew, but that is not enough. Did you

ever think of the origin of the word *avarice?*'

'No.'

'It comes – at least it seems top me to come – from the same root as the verb to *have*, and holds relation with anything. It is the desire to call *things* ours – the desire of company which is not of our kind – company such as, is small enough, you would put in your pocket and carry round with you. We call the holding in the hand, or the house, or the pocket, or the power, *having*; but such things cannot really be *had. Having* is but an illusion in regard to *things.* It is only what we can be *with* that we really possess – that is, what is our kind, from God to the lowest animal partaking of humanity. A love can never be lost. It is a possession. But who can take his diamond ring into the somewhere beyond? It is not a possession. God can only be ours perfectly; nothing called property can be ours at all.' [72]

Dorothy L. Sayers (1893-1957)

A novelist, dramatist, essayist, translator and scholar, Dorothy L. Sayers is best known for her detective novels featuring the laconic aristocratic Lord Peter Wimsey, and for her ground-breaking radio plays on the life of Christ, *Man Born to be King.* On 23 October 1941, while Britain was at war, she addressed the Public Morality Council on the subject of 'The Other Six Deadly Sins', introducing her subject with an anecdote about a young man who once said to her, 'I did not know there were seven deadly sins: please tell me the names of the other six.'

Sayers equates avarice with the twentieth-century enthusiasm for 'enterprise', and points out, with typical wit and pungency, that it is a national sin in which we all collude.

Let us ask ourselves one or two questions. Do we admire and envy rich people because they are rich, or because the work by which they made their money is good work? If we hear that Old So-and-So has pulled off a pretty smart deal with the Town Council, are we shocked by the revelation of the cunning graft involved, or do we say admiringly: 'Old So-and-So's hot stuff – you won't find many flies on him'? When we go to the cinema and see a picture about empty-headed people in luxurious surroundings, do we say 'What drivel!' or do we sit in a misty dream, wishing we could give up our daily work and marry into surroundings like that? When we invest our money, do we ask ourselves whether the enterprise represents anything useful, or merely whether it is a safe thing that returns a good dividend? Do we regularly put money into football pools or dog-racing? When we read the newspaper, are our eyes immediately arrested by anything which says 'MILLIONS' in large capitals, preceded by the £ or $ sign? Have we ever refused money on the grounds that the work that we had to do for it was something that we could not do honestly, or do well? Do we NEVER choose our acquaintance with the idea that they are useful people to know, or keep in with people in the hope that there is something to be got out of them? And do we – this is important – when we blame the mess that the economical world has got into, do we always lay the blame on wicked financiers, wicked profiteers, wicked capitalists, wicked employers, wicked bankers – or do we sometimes ask ourselves how far *we* have contributed to make the mess?

Just as the sin of Gluttony thrives on our little greeds, so the sin of Covetousness thrives on our little acts of avarice ... We are all in it together.[73]

Sloth

Then came Sloth, all slobbered and sticky-eyed. 'I must sit down,' he said, 'or I'll fall asleep. I can't stand and I can't stoop – I can't even kneel without a footstool. Put me to bed and – unless my bowels make me get up – there isn't a church bell whose ringing would make me rise before dinner-time.'

Then, with a belch and beating of his breast, he launched into the *Benedicite*. Then he stretched, yawned and finally snored.'[74]

Jerome K. Jerome (1859-1927)

The author of *Three Men in a Boat* also wrote *The Idle Thoughts of an Idle Fellow: A Book For an Idle Holiday* (1889) and founded (in 1892) the *Idler* magazine. Obviously an authority on sloth! Among his wise comments on the matter are, 'It is impossible to enjoy idling thoroughly unless one has plenty of work to be do.'

I like idling when I ought not to be idling; not when it is the only thing I have to do. That is my pig-headed nature. The time I like best to stand with my back to the fire, calculating how much I owe, is when my desk is heaped highest with letters that must be answered by the next post. When I like to dawdle longest over my dinner, is when I have a heavy evening's work before me. And if, for some urgent reason, I ought to be up particularly early in the morning, it is then, more than at any other time, that I love to lie an extra half-hour in bed.[75]

Of course there is a serious side – you might say a 'deadly' serious side – to sloth. As Dorothy L. Sayers remarks:

'We have known it far too well for many years. The only thing perhaps that we have not known about it is that it is mortal sin.[76]

Theologically, sloth is defined as 'being careless towards the things of God' – a sin that combines neglect of one's own spiritual welfare with contempt for the gospel, all in the hope that there will be time enough when one is old to get oneself right with God. Spiritual sloth of this kind was a favourite theme with the writers of Victorian evangelical novelists, one of whose recurrent topics was The Sinner Who Left It Too Late.

Talbot Baines Reed (1853-1893)

Reed is best known for his novels of school life, but he also wrote short stories, some of which are contained in his collection of character sketches, *Parkhurst Boys*. Among them is the salutary tale, 'The Troubles of a Dawdler'. It is not one of Reed's most successful pieces of storytelling, probably because on this occasion he came to his writing desk with a sermon ready to preach. Here is how the story ends.

I must pass over the next two years [having wasted his school years through idleness he is now wasting opportunities of rewarding employment] and come to the conclusion of my story. During those two years I entered upon and left no less than three employments – each less advantageous than the former. The end of that time found me a clerk in a bank in a country town. In this capacity my besetting sin was still haunting me. I had several times been called into the manager's room, and reprimanded for unpunctuality, or cautioned for wasting my time. The few friends who on my first coming to the town had taken an interest in me had dropped away, disgusted at my unreliable conduct, or because I myself had neglected their acquaintance. My employers had ceased to entrust me with any commissions requiring promptitude or care; and I was nothing more than an office drudge – and a very unprofitable drudge too. Such was my condition when, one morning, a telegram reached me from my mother to say –

'Father is very ill. Come at once.'

I was shocked at this bad news, and determined to start for London by the next train ... By the time I had made up my mind which to take, and enquired where a lad could be found who would carry my portmanteau to the station, it was too late to catch the train, and I therefore had three hours to spare before I could leave. This delay, in my anxious condition, worried me, and I was at a loss how to occupy the interval. If I had been wise, I should never have quitted that station till I did so in the train. But alas! I decided to take a stroll instead. It was a sad walk, for my father's image was constantly before my eyes, and I could hardly bear to think of his being ill. I thought of all his goodness and forbearance to me, and wondered what would become of us if he were not to recover. I wandered on, broken-hearted, and repenting deeply of all my ingratitude, and the ill return I had made him for his love to me, and I looked forward eagerly to being able to throw myself in his arms once more, and beg his forgiveness.

Thus I mused far into the morning, when it occurred to me to look at my watch. Was it possible? It wanted not half an hour of the time for the train, and I was more than two miles from the place. I started to walk rapidly, and soon came in sight of the town. What fatal madness impelled me at that moment to stand and look at a ploughing match that was taking place in a field by the roadside? For a minute or two my anxiety, my father, the train, all were forgotten in the excitement of that contest. Then I recovered myself and dashed on like the wind. Once more (as I thought but for an instant) I paused to examine a gypsy encampment on the border of the wood, and then, reminded by a distant whistle, hurried forward. Alas! As I dashed into the station the train was slowly turning the corner and I sunk down in an agony of despair and humiliation.

* * *

When I reached home at midnight, my mother met me at the door.

'Well, you are come at last,' she said quietly.

'Come and see him.'

I sprang up the stairs beside her. She opened the door softly, and bade me enter.

My father lay there dead.

'He waited for you all day,' said my mother, 'and died not an hour ago. His last words were, "Charlie is late." Oh, Charlie, why did you not come sooner?'

Then she knelt with me beside my dead father. And, in that dark lonely chamber, that night, the turning-point of my life was reached.

* * *

Boys, I am an old man now; but, believe me, since that awful moment I have never, to my knowledge, dawdled again![77]

Geoffrey Hill (b. 1932)

Hill is regarded by some critics as the most distinguished poet in the English language since T.S. Eliot. His poetry deals with central themes of human history and spiritual experience. His sequence of sonnets *Lachrimae* culminates in an exquisitely perceived meditation on spiritual sloth, in the sonnet 'Lachrimae Amantis'.

What is there in my heart that you should sue
so fiercely for its love? What kind of care
brings you as though a stranger to my door
through the long night and in the icy dew

seeking the heart that will not harbour you,
that keeps itself religiously secure?
At this dark solstice filled with frost and fire
your passion's ancient wounds must bleed anew.

So many nights the angel of my house
has fed such urgent comfort through a dream,
whispered 'your Lord is coming, he is close'

that I have drowsed half-faithful for a time
bathed in pure tones of promise and remorse:
'tomorrow I shall wake to welcome him.'[78]

John Berryman (1914-1972)

On the other side of the Atlantic, John Berryman, a generation earlier than Geoffrey Hill, achieved similar distinction, as one of America's leading poets. His poetry (especially the very long sequence of sonnets beginning in 1955 with *His Toy His Dream His Rest*) charts unsparingly his own tempestuous life, and records recurrent religious reflections which came to resolution in the moving collection *Love and Fame* (1970). The almost conversational 'Eleven Addresses to the Lord' seem to record a confession of a lifetime of spiritual sloth, culminating finally in spiritual commitment. The eleven poems in the sequence present a very different picture to the implicit spiritual tragedy of Hill's *Tenebrae* sequence.

... You have come to my rescue again & again
in my impassable, sometimes despairing years.

You have allowed my brilliant friends
    to destroy themselves
and I am still here, severely damaged,
    but functioning.

Unknowable, as I am unknown to my
    guinea pigs:
how can I 'love' you?
I only as far as gratitude & awe
confidently & absolutely go.... [79]

Isaac Watts (1674-1748)

The dangers of spiritual sloth and neglect of one's eternal well-being led (in a much earlier age) Isaac Watts – an Independent pastor and author of over 600 hymns – to bend his creative gifts to writing 'Moral Songs' that would deliver children from 'the Temptation of Loving or Learning those Idle, Wanton or Profane Songs, which give so early an ill Taint to the Fancy and Memory, and become the Seeds of future Vices'. Most conscientious parents of that time would impress verses like the following – 'The Sluggard' – upon their offspring, hoping for virtuous results and a determination to turn away from, among other vices, sloth:

'Tis the Voice of the *Sluggard*. I heard him complain
You have wak'd me too soon, I must slumber again.
As the door on its Hinges, so he on his Bed,
Turns his Sides, and his Shoulders, and his heavy Head.

A little more Sleep, and a little more Slumber;
Thus he wast's half his Days, and his Hours
    without number;
And when he gets up, he sits folding his Hands
Or walks about saunt'ring, or trifling he stands.

I past by his Garden, and saw the wild Briar
The Thorn and the Thistle grow broader and higher;
The Clothes that hang on him are turning to Rags;
And his Money still wast's, still he starves, or he begs.

I made him a Visit, still hoping to find
He had took better care for improving his Mind:
He told me his Dreams, talk'd of eating and drinking,
But he scarce reads his Bible, and never loves thinking.

Said I then to my Heart, *Here's a Lesson for me,*
That Man's but the Picture of what I might be:
But thanks to my Friends for their care in my Breeding:
Who taught me betimes to love Working and Reading.[80]

Lewis Carroll
(The Rev Charles Lutwidge Dodgson, 1832-1898)

You may be wondering, not surprisingly, where you heard
those lines before. One hundred and fifty years later, the
author of *Alice in Wonderland*, himself a man of the cloth,
mercilessly parodied them in that story.

'Tis the voice of the Lobster: I heard him declare,
'You have baked me too brown, I must sugar my hair.'
As a duck with his eyelids, so he with his nose
Trims his belt and his buttons, and turns out his toes.
When the sands are all dry, he is gay as a lark,
And will talk in contemptuous tones of the Shark:
But, when the tide rises and sharks are around,
His voice has a timid and tremulous sound.

I passed by his garden, and marked with one eye,
How the Owl and the Panther were sharing a pie:

The Panther took pie-crust, and gravy, and meat,
While the Owl had the dish as its share of the treat.
When the pie was all finished, the Owl, as a boon,
Was kindly permitted to pocket the spoon:
While the Panther received knife and fork with a growl,
And concluded the banquet by – [81]

At which point Lewis Carroll draws a polite veil.

It was admittedly a *very* comprehensive destruction of Watts's Moral Song, but in Carroll's defence it must be acknowledged that earlier in the same book he had created one of the truly memorable examples of – if not sloth, then certainly extreme tiredness:

> 'You should say what you mean,' the March Hare went on.
>
> 'I do,' Alice hastily replied, 'at least – at least I mean what I say – that's the same thing, you know.'
>
> 'Not the same thing a bit!' said the Hatter. 'Why, you might just as well say that "I see what I eat" is the same thing as "I eat what I see"!'
>
> 'You might just as well say,' added the March Hare, 'that "I like what I get" is the same thing as "I get what I like"!'
>
> 'You might just as well say,' added the Dormouse, which seemed to be talking in its sleep, 'that "I breathe when I sleep" is the same thing as "I sleep when I breathe"!'
>
> 'It *is* the same thing with you,' said the Hatter, and here the conversation dropped.[82]

William Law (1686-1761)

There can't be many books with titles so deceptively dull as William Law's *A Serious Call to a Devout and Holy Life*, for this superbly written, razor-sharp call to a life of piety is rich with wit and some devastatingly perceptive character studies. Law makes us see that sloth is not simply a sin but a symptom; for Law, who studied to become a clergyman but was deprived of any employment in the church because of his political convictions, sloth indicated a deeply flawed relationship with God.

Here is Flavia, who displays most of the deadly sins and none of the seven virtues.

Flavia is very idle, and yet very fond of fine work: this makes her often sit working in bed until noon, and be told many a long story before she is up; so that I need not tell you, that her morning devotions are not always rightly performed.

Flavia would be a miracle of Piety, if she was but half so careful of her soul, as she is of her body. The rising of a pimple in her face, the sting of a gnat, will make her keep her room two or three days, and she thinks they are very rash people, that don't take care of things in time. This makes her so over-careful of her health, that she never thinks she is well enough; and so over indulgent, that she can never be really well. So that it costs her a great deal in sleeping-draughts and waking-draughts, in spirits for the head, in drops for the nerves, in cordials for the stomach, and in saffron for the tea.

If you visit Flavia on the Sunday, you will always meet good company, you will know what is going on in the world, you will hear the last lampoon, you will be told who wrote it, and who is meant by every name that is in it ... Flavia thinks they are Atheists that play at cards on the Sunday, but she will tell you the nicety of all the games, what cards she held, how she play'd them, and the history of all that happened at play, as soon as she comes from Church ... If you would know how cross Lucius is to his wife ... how they hate one another in their hearts, tho' they appear so kind in publick; you must visit Flavia on the Sunday. But still she has so great a regard for the holiness of the Sunday, that she has turned a poor old widow out of her house, as a profane wretch, for having been found once mending her clothes on the Sunday night.

Thus lives Flavia; and if she lives ten years longer, she will have spent about fifteen hundred and sixty Sundays after this manner. She will have wore about two hundred different suits of clothes. Out of this thirty years of her life, fifteen of them will have been disposed of in bed; and of the remaining fifteen, about fourteen of them will have been consumed in eating, drinking, dressing, visiting, conversation, reading and hearing Plays and Romances, at Operas, Assemblies, Balls and Diversions. For you may reckon all the time that she is up, thus spent, except about an hour and a half, that is disposed of at Church, most Sundays in the year. With great management, and under mighty rules of economy, she will have spent sixty hundred pounds upon herself, bating only some shilling, crowns, or half-crowns, that have gone from her in accidental charities.

I shall not take it upon me to say, that it is impossible for Flavia to be saved; but thus much must be said, that she has no grounds from Scripture to think she is in the way of salvation. For her whole life is in direct opposition to all those tempers and practices, which the Gospel has made necessary to salvation.[83]

Robert South (1634-1716)

As we have seen, sloth was originally defined as a religious error. As such it is seen most dramatically in church!

Robert South encountered it even when when preaching a royal sermon:

> 'Lord Lauderdale, let me entreat you to rouse yourself; you snore so loud that you will wake the King!'

C.H. Spurgeon (1834-1892)

The celebrated preacher Charles Haddon Spurgeon was also one of the wittiest of writers – his *Lectures to My Students* are a treasure-trove of quotable quotes. In Lecture IX (series 1), entitled 'Attention!', he makes the point at great length that if the congregation sleeps it is usually the preacher's fault. Here is one of his many illustrations:

> The minister who recommended the old lady to take snuff in order to keep from dozing was very properly rebuked by her reply – that if he would put more snuff into the sermon she would be awake enough.

Spurgeon issues a strong warning to his students that if the congregation sleeps the preacher might as well do so too. Which recalls the story (probably, unfortunately, apocryphal) of the Archbishop of Canterbury who dreamed he was preaching the Easter sermon at Canterbury Cathedral – and woke up to find that he was.

Idle Remarks

While we're in the mood for slothful soundbites, here are a few more!

> Lying in bed would be an altogether perfect and supreme experience if only one had a coloured pencil long enough to draw on the ceiling.
>
> (G.K. Chesterton, 1874-1936)

> To spend too much time in studies is sloth.
>
> (Francis Bacon, 1561-1626)

For even when we were with you, we gave you this rule: 'If a man will not work, he shall not eat.'
(St Paul, writing to the Thessalonian Church)

As writers become more numerous, it is natural for readers to become more indolent.
(Oliver Goldsmith, 1728-1774)

Surely, surely, slumber is more sweet than toil, the shore
Than labour in the deep mid-ocean, wind and wave and oar;
Oh rest ye, brother mariners, we will not wander more.
(Alfred, Lord Tennyson, 1809-1892)

The Book of Proverbs

The classic picture of sloth, drawing on all the aspects of the word that we have been looking at, is found in that ancient book of pithy wisdom, the Book of Proverbs. With this very well-known passage we conclude our survey of the seven deadly sins.

> Go to the ant, you sluggard; consider its ways and be wise!
> It has no commander, no overseer or ruler,
> yet it stores its provisions in summer and gathers its food at harvest.
> How long will you lie there, you sluggard?
> When will you get up from your sleep?
> A little sleep, a little slumber, a little folding of the hands to rest –
> and poverty will come on you like a bandit
> and scarcity like an armed man.[84]

Part II
The Seven Virtues

The Theological Virtues

Whereas the seven deadly sins are a single list, the seven virtues are subdivided. The first three – Faith, Hope and Love – are known as the 'theological', 'supernatural' or 'Christian' virtues. They are taken from St Paul's eloquent words in 1 Corinthians 13, which are quoted here in the memorable rendering of the Authorised Version of the Bible (where 'love' is translated 'charity'):

St Paul

> Though I speak with the tongues of men and of angels, and have not charity, I am become *as* sounding brass, or a tinkling cymbal. And though I have *the gift of* prophecy, and understand all mysteries, and all knowledge; and though I have all faith, so that I could remove mountains, and have not charity, I am nothing. And though I bestow all my goods to feed *the poor*, and though I give my body to be burned, and have not charity, it profiteth me nothing.
>
> Charity suffereth long, *and* is kind; charity envieth not; charity vaunteth not itself, is not puffed up, Doth not behave itself unseemly, seeketh not her own, is not easily provoked, thinketh no evil; Rejoiceth not in iniquity, but rejoiceth in the truth; Beareth all things, believeth all things, hopeth all things, endureth all things.
>
> Charity never faileth: but whether *there be* prophecies, they shall fail; whether *there be* tongues, they shall cease; whether *there be* knowledge, it shall vanish away. For we know in part, and we prophesy in part. But when that which is perfect is come, then that which is in part shall be done away. When I was a child, I spake as a child, I understood as a child, I thought as a child: but when I became a man, I put

away childish things. For now we see through a glass, darkly; but then face to face: now I know in part; but then shall I know even as also I am known. And now abideth faith, hope, charity, these three; but the greatest of these *is* charity.[85]

They are called 'theological virtues' because you cannot develop them by an effort of will or by conscientious self-discipline. You cannot, the medieval Church pointed out, acquire them through your own initiative. Only God can put faith in your heart; only God can put hope in your heart; only God can put love in your heart. The doctrine of the fall affirms that left to their own devices, human beings will tend to disbelieve rather than trust, to despair rather than hope, to hate rather than love. And the queen of the theological virtues is love, the Church taught.

> To describe a virtue as 'natural' is to say that it is humanly conceived and acquired (no matter how fundamental it may be for the moral ordering of a soul or a society). To describe a virtue as 'theological' is to say that its distinctive quality as a virtue is rooted in the character of God and that it has been revealed, and may be bestowed, by God alone. While all virtues are settled, strong, inner dispositions or tendencies, natural virtues may be acquired through self-discipline and training, and theological ones are gifts of God inseparable from the presence of God in the life of the redeemed. Augustine concluded that since the natural virtues have no reference to God, they are not true virtues at all but 'splendid vices'. Thomas Aquinas, on the other hand, separates the theological virtues from the natural virtues.[86]

Perhaps because the counterpart to the seven deadly sins are not seven virtues but three plus four virtues, they do not neatly complement each other. Though lust is a deadly sin, chastity is not singled out as one of the virtues, neither is sloth matched by industry. On the other hand, lust and gluttony are matched by temperance.

There are several likely reasons why the vices and virtues are so imperfectly matched. One is certainly that defining a vice as a deadly sin might well be regarded as defining its opposite as a virtue and vice versa. Another is that the vices and virtues were not intended to be clear-cut lists anyway; they were convenient identifiers for the range of human strengths and weaknesses, and each one of them irresistibly calls others to mind. That is one reason why they have become effective shorthand in many religious and secular contexts, and why in a sense to mention one is to mention them all.

Walter Savage Landor (1775-1864)

Here is Walter Savage Landor, allowing a selection to speak for the whole:

> Around the child bend all the three
> Sweet Graces: Faith, Hope, Charity.
> Around the man bend other faces:
> Pride, Envy, Malice, are his graces.[87]

Faith

The Book of Jeremiah

If you step on a frozen lake you need to have faith that the ice will bear you up. If your trust in the ice only exists when you have safely walked across the ice, it is not faith but knowledge.

Faith is a biblical virtue, and one of the most striking examples of faith is in the Old Testament, where Jeremiah, his nation at the point of catastrophe and his own fate likely to be exile or worse, chooses that very moment to invest in real estate.

> The word of the LORD came to me: Hanamel son of Shallum your uncle is going to come to you and say, 'Buy my field at Anathoth, because as nearest relative it is your right and duty to buy it.' Then, just as the LORD had said, my cousin Hanamel came to me in the courtyard of the guard and said, 'Buy my field at Anathoth in the territory of Benjamin. Since it is your right to redeem it and possess it, buy it for yourself.' "I knew that this was the word of the LORD; so I bought the field at Anathoth from my cousin Hanamel and weighed out for him seventeen shekels of silver. I signed and sealed the deed, had it witnessed, and weighed out the silver on the scales. I took the deed of purchase – the sealed copy containing the terms and conditions, as well as the unsealed copy – and I gave this deed to Baruch son of Neriah, the son of Mahseiah, in the presence of my cousin Hanamel and of the witnesses who had signed the deed and of all the Jews sitting in the courtyard of the guard.
>
> In their presence I gave Baruch these instructions: 'This is what the LORD Almighty, the God of Israel,

says: Take these documents, both the sealed and unsealed copies of the deed of purchase, and put them in a clay jar so that they will last a long time. For this is what the LORD Almighty, the God of Israel, says: Houses, fields and vineyards will again be bought in this land.'

After I had given the deed of purchase to Baruch son of Neriah, I prayed to the LORD: 'Ah, Sovereign LORD, you have made the heavens and the earth by your great power and outstretched arm. Nothing is too hard for you. You show love to thousands but bring the punishment for the fathers' sins into the laps of their children after them. O great and powerful God, whose name is the LORD Almighty, great are your purposes and mighty are your deeds. Your eyes are open to all the ways of men; you reward everyone according to his conduct and as his deeds deserve. You performed miraculous signs and wonders in Egypt and have continued them to this day, both in Israel and among all mankind, and have gained the renown that is still yours. You brought your people Israel out of Egypt with signs and wonders, by a mighty hand and an outstretched arm and with great terror. You gave them this land you had sworn to give to their forefathers, a land flowing with milk and honey. They came in and took possession of it, but they did not obey you or follow your law; they did not do what you commanded them to do. So you brought all this disaster upon them.

'See how the siege ramps are built up to take the city. Because of the sword, famine and plague, the city will be handed over to the Babylonians who are attacking it. What you said has happened, as you now see. And though the city will be handed over to the Babylonians, you, O Sovereign LORD, say to me, 'Buy the field with silver and have the transaction witnessed.'

Then the word of the LORD came to Jeremiah: 'I am the LORD, the God of all mankind. Is anything too hard for me? ... As I have brought all this great calamity on this people, so I will give them all the prosperity I have promised them. Once more fields will be bought in this land of which you say, "It is a desolate waste, without men or animals, for it has been handed over to the Babylonians." Fields will be bought for silver, and deeds will be signed, sealed and witnessed in the territory of Benjamin, in the villages around Jerusalem, in the towns of Judah and in the towns of the hill country, of the western foothills and of the Negev, because I will restore their fortunes, declares the LORD.' [88]

Faith is a virtue that has something of the child-like about it. That does not mean that it is only for children, simply that often children are better at it. Jesus made a point of crediting children with strong faith in the kingdom he came to preach:

Jesus called the children to him and said, 'Let the little children come to me, and do not hinder them, for the kingdom of God belongs to such as these. I tell you the truth, anyone who will not receive the kingdom of God like a little child will never enter it.' [89]

Richard Wurmbrand (b. 1909)

Richard Wurmbrand, a Romanian Jewish pastor, became known in the West when his sufferings during fourteen years in communist prisons were publicised. His account of those years, *Tortured for Christ* (1967), is a modern classic of suffering for faith. He is the author of many other books, including a collection of anecdotes about children and their faith, in which he tells the following story:

I was able to take [Mihai, his son] to the toy shop. At that time the Soviet army had just invaded Rumania, our homeland, and had shown a marked liking for alcohol. A great deal of drunkenness was in evidence.

When we entered the department store, a Soviet captain was there with a woman sergeant. They were attempting to make some purchases, but were handicapped by not knowing our language, On the other hand, the salesman could not speak Russian. I offered to translate for them.

Mihai repeatedly urged me to tell them about Christ. I too was waiting for the right moment.

After I had helped them in their spending spree, the sergeant said to me, 'You have been so kind to us. Perhaps you could do me one more favour. I need some dresses. Where can I find them?'

Now I knew she was at my mercy!

'I haven't the slightest idea about such matters – but may I invite the captain and you to come to our home for lunch? Afterwards, my wife will take you shopping.'

Mihai was delighted that we would have them in our home, where they could learn about the faith. 'Buy them a bottle of wine,' he urged. 'Then they'll listen better. You know that all their soldiers are drunkards!'

Probably he had heard me quote Paul's words: 'To the Jews I became like a Jew, to win the Jews ... To the weak I became weak, to win the weak' (1 Cor. 9:20,22). I smiled at his ingenuous suggestion; but I was indeed able to share with my guests the fruit of the True Vine, which gives life eternal.

Both officers were converted.[90]

The Epistle to the Hebrews

For a definition of faith – and some historical examples – we can turn to the author of the New Testament letter to the Hebrews, and the long catalogue of the faithful throughout history.

Now faith is being sure of what we hope for and certain of what we do not see. This is what the ancients were commended for.

By faith we understand that the universe was formed at God's command, so that what is seen was not made out of what was visible ...

By faith Noah, when warned about things not yet seen, in holy fear built an ark to save his family. By his faith he condemned the world and became heir of the righteousness that comes by faith.

By faith Abraham, when called to go to a place he would later receive as his inheritance, obeyed and went, even though he did not know where he was going. By faith he made his home in the promised land like a stranger in a foreign country; he lived in tents, as did Isaac and Jacob, who were heirs with him of the same promise. For he was looking forward to the city with foundations, whose architect and builder is God ...

All these people were still living by faith when they died. They did not receive the things promised; they only saw them and welcomed them from a distance. And they admitted that they were aliens and strangers on earth. People who say such things show that they are looking for a country of their own. If they had been thinking of the country they had left, they would have had opportunity to return. Instead, they were longing for a better country—a heavenly one. Therefore God is not ashamed to be called their God, for he has prepared a city for them ...

And what more shall I say? I do not have time to tell about Gideon, Barak, Samson, Jephthah, David, Samuel and the prophets, who through faith conquered kingdoms, administered justice, and gained what was promised; who shut the mouths of lions, quenched the fury of the flames, and escaped the edge of the sword; whose weakness was turned to strength; and who became powerful in battle and routed foreign armies. Women received back their dead, raised to life again. Others were tortured and refused to be released, so that they might gain a better resurrection. Some faced jeers and flogging, while still others were chained and put in prison. They were stoned; they were sawn in two; they were put to death by the sword. They went about in sheepskins and goatskins, destitute, persecuted and ill-treated – the world was not worthy of them. They wandered in deserts and mountains, and in caves and holes in the ground.

These were all commended for their faith, yet none of them received what had been promised.[91]

William Blake (1757-1827)

Blake was a poet of rare vision who, in *The Marriage of Heaven and Hell*, attacked the 'angels' who fed the people images of a fearful hell and a dreary heaven. It is a savage satire by a man who holds on to his own faith and hope in the face of the dire warnings of prophetical doomsayers – and his own conviction that the apocalypse might be just around the corner. The following 'Memorable Fancy', illustrating his total trust in his own perception of truth against all the odds, was used by P.D. James in her detective novel *No Job for a Woman*, where it forms the text of a moving suicide note.

An Angel came to me and said, 'O pitiable foolish young man! O horrible! O dreadful state! Consider the hot burning dungeon thou art preparing for thyself to all eternity, to which thou art going in such career.'

I said, 'Perhaps you will be willing to shew me my eternal lot, & we will contemplate together upon it, and see whether your lot or mine is most desirable.'

So he took me thro' a stable & thro' a church & down into the church vault, at the end of which was a mill: thro' the mill we went, and came to a cave: down the winding cavern we groped our tedious way, till a void boundless as a nether sky appear'd beneath us, & we held by the roots of trees and hung over this immensity; but I said: 'if you please, we will commit ourselves to this void, and see whether providence is here also: if you will not, I will.' [92]

Francis A. Schaeffer (1912-1984)

For Blake, his own knowledge of providence was a better ground for faith than the 'angel' who would mislead him.

True faith is not blind faith, though there is no human act that does not require a prior faith-commitment in some shape or form. For example, the scientist operates on the basis of the uniformity of cause in a predictable universe; and though there is no absolute reason for the sun to appear tomorrow, we assume that it will, and it is a reasonable assumption, given what we know of the sun's behaviour so far.

But the faith that irrationally believes in something or someone out of hopelessness, sentimentality or ignorance is not faith at all. Here is Francis Schaeffer, who for many years wrote of, and taught, the relevance of historic Christianity to twentieth-century culture, talking about a very similar situation to that described by Blake:

Suppose we are climbing in the Alps and are very high on the bare rock, and suddenly the fog shuts down. The guide turns to us and says that the ice is forming and that there is no hope; before morning we will all freeze to death here on the shoulder of the mountain. Simply to keep warm the guide keeps us moving in the dense fog further out on the shoulder until none of us have any idea where we are. After an hour or so, someone says to the guide, 'Suppose I dropped and hit a ledge ten feet down in the fog. What would happen then? The guide would say that you might make it until the morning and thus live. So, with absolutely no knowledge or any reason to support his action, one of the group hangs and drops into the fog. This would be one kind of faith, a leap of faith.

Suppose, however, after we have worked out on the shoulder in the midst of the fog and the growing ice on the rock, we had stopped and we heard a voice which said, 'You cannot see me, but I know exactly where you are from your voices. I am on another ridge. I have lived on these mountains, man and boy, for over sixty years and I know every foot of them. I assure you that ten feet below you there is a ledge. If you hang and drop, you can make it through the night and I will get you in the morning.'

I would not hang and drop at once, but would ask questions to try to ascertain if the man knew what he was talking about and if he was not my enemy. In the Alps, for example, I would ask him his name. If the name he gave me was the name of a family from that part of the mountains, it would count a great deal to me ... In my desperate situation, even though time would be running out, I would ask him what to me would be the adequate and sufficient questions, and when I became convinced by his answers, then I would hang and drop.

This is faith, but obviously it has no relationship to the other use of the word. As a matter of fact, if one of these is called faith, the other should not be designated by the same word.[93]

Hope

The second of the three 'theological virtues' has various meanings in traditional Christianity. In creeds and confessions, Jesus Christ is the believer's 'hope' on whom their acts of hope are founded. But hope is also an attitude of mind, an expectation and a confidence. That is why hope is regarded as a virtue; you can only have it, in the sense in which the Bible speaks of it, if you have faith; if you believe in the Source of hope. That is the kind of hope that inspired Julian of Norwich to write the words (which T.S. Eliot quotes in his Christian meditative poems *Four Quartets*), 'All shall be well'. In the *Revelations of Divine Love*, Julian sets out the right relationship between sin and hope.

Julian of Norwich (died c.1443)

After this the Lord brought to my mind the longing that I had to Him afore. And I saw that nothing hindered me but sin. And so I looked, generally, upon us all, and methought: *If sin had not been, we should all have been clean and like to our Lord, as He made us.*

And thus, in my folly, afore this time often I wondered why by the great foreseeing wisdom of God the beginning of sin was not hindered: for then, methought, all should have been well. This stirring of mind was much to be forsaken, but nevertheless mourning and sorrow I made therefor, without reason and discretion.

But Jesus, who in this Vision informed me of all that is needful to me, answered by this word and said: It behoved that there should be sin; but all shall be well, and all shall be well, and all manner of thing shall be well....

And thus pain, it is something, as to my sight, for a time; for it purgeth, and maketh us to know ourselves and to ask mercy. For the Passion of our Lord is comfort to us against all this, and so is His blessed will. And for the tender love that our good Lord hath to all that shall be saved, He comforteth readily and sweetly, signifying thus: It is true that sin is cause of all this pain; but all shall be well, and all shall be well, and all manner of thing shall be well.[94]

Alfred, Lord Tennyson (1809-1892)

The great Victorian poet Tennyson was a spokesman for the beliefs and values of his generation, and like Kipling later, he often celebrated the empire, the Crown and colonial conquest in poems that confidently associate God's will with the lands on which the sun never set – a triumphalism that few today find acceptable, let alone biblical. But in his well-known anthem 'Crossing the Bar', published in 1892 and written in old age, Tennyson strikes a simpler note of quiet devotion, in a hymn of hope that reflects a certainty absent from modern life.

A 'bar' is, in sailing terms, a submerged sand bank or other underwater hazard that prevents a navigational problem; so sailing into the dark calls for a skilled pilot who knows those waters from experience – the ageing Tennyson's symbolism is not difficult to work out.

Sunset and evening star,
    And one clear call for me!
And may there be no moaning of the bar
    When I put out to sea,

But such a tide as moving seems asleep,
    Too full for sound and foam,
When that which drew from out the boundless deep
    Turns again home.

Twilight and evening bell,
    And after that the dark!
And may there be no sadness of farewell,
    When I embark;

For tho' from out our bourne of Time and Place
    The flood may bear me far,
I hope to see my Pilot face to face
    When I have crost the bar.

When hope is broadened to embrace the future of mankind
it often takes on the look of a religious or political agenda.
Tennyson managed to combine both in his long poem
Locksley Hall [95], with its vision of a future hope: commerce,
blessed by human labour and a benevolent God:

Men, my brothers, men the workers, ever reaping
    something new:
That which they have done but earnest of the things
    that they shall do;

For I dipt into the future, far as human eye could see,
Saw the Vision of the world, and all the wonder that
    would be;

Saw the heavens fill with commerce, argosies of magic
    sails,
Pilots of the purple twilight, dropping down with
    costly bales;

Heard the heavens fill with shouting, and there rain'd
    a ghastly dew
From the nations' airy navies grappling in the central
    blue;

Far along the world-wide whisper of the south-wind
    rushing warm,
With the standards of the people plunging thro' the
    thunder-storm;

Till the war-drum throbb'd no longer, and the battle-
flags were furled
In the Parliament of man, the Federation of the
world.

There the common sense of most shall hold a fretful
realm in awe,
And the kindly earth shall slumber, lapt in universal
law.

Tennyson's future Utopia is not to be won without a fight,
and his 'airy navies' were a remarkable prophetic vision of
the twentieth-century air warfare. He was not the only
prophet who had great hopes for the future of the world but
few illusions about human nature.

H.G. Wells (1866-1946)

Wells was a novelist and political philosopher, whose
science fiction has been made into several films. He
foresaw accurately much twentieth-century scientific
innovation, but also depicted graphically the kind of war
and suffering that science brings along with its benefits. In
the closing pages of *The Time Machine* (1895) the Traveller,
having related his experiences of travelling through time,
goes back on his travels, leaving his friend to contemplate
what he has heard and to speculate on what hopes exist for
humanity.

> One cannot choose but wonder. Will he ever return?
> It may be that he swept back into the past, and fell
> among the blood-drinking, hairy savages of the Age of
> Unpolished Stone; into the abysses of the Cretaceous
> Sea; or among the grotesque saurians, the huge
> reptilian brutes of the Jurassic times. He may be even
> now – if I may use the phrase – be wandering on some
> plesiosaurus-haunted Oolitic coral reef, or beside the

lonely saline lakes of the Triassic Age. Or did he go forward, into one of the nearer ages, in which men are still men, but with the riddles of our own time answered and its wearisome problems solved? Into the manhood of the race: for I, for my own part, cannot think that these latter days of weak experiment, fragmentary theory, and mutual discord are indeed man's culminating time! I say, for my own part. He, I know – for the question had been discussed among us long before the Time Machine was made – thought but cheerlessly of the Advancement of Mankind, and saw in the growing pile of civilisation only a foolish heaping that must inevitably fall back upon and destroy its makers in the end. If that is so, it remains for us to live as though it were not so. But to me the future is still bleak and blank – is a vast ignorance, lit at a few casual places by the memory of his story. And I have by me, for my comfort, two strange white flowers – shrivelled now, and brown and flat and brittle – to witness that even when mind and strength had gone, gratitude and a mutual tenderness still lived on in the heart of man.[96]

Wells, who lived through two world wars, was aware that optimism must be cautious and that whatever was precious and humane in human beings coexisted with a capability for immense evil. So his vision of the future was not belief in an inevitable social perfectionism.

William Morris (1834-1896)

A socialist of a very different type was William Morris, whose hope for the future embraced a society purged of oppression and injustice, in which the ugliness of nineteenth-century industrialism would be swept away and replaced by a largely rural economy in which everybody had enough and to spare. In such a society, men and women would no longer use money. People would work only if and because they wanted to, and if anybody were in need, those who had enough would share their good fortune. In his novel *News From Nowhere: a Utopian Romance* (1891) a resident of Victorian London falls asleep and awakes in a socialist commonwealth, flourishing in an England of the distant future. There he finds many people who are more than ready to show him round and act as mouthpieces for Morris's central creed; that it is labour and sorrow that make mankind bad; take away their chains and their burdens, and they will become good.

> We came just here on a gang of men road-mending, which delayed us a little; but I was not sorry for it; for all I had seen hitherto had seemed part of a summer holiday; and I wanted to see how this folk would set to on a piece of real necessary work. They had been resting, and had only just begun work again as we came up; so that the rattle of picks was what woke me from my musing. There were about a dozen of them, strong young men, looking much like a boating party in Oxford would have looked in the days I remembered, and not more troubled with their work: their outer raiment lay on the road-side in an orderly pile under the guardianship of a six-year- old boy, who had his arm thrown over the neck of a big mastiff, who was as happily lazy as if the summer day had been made for him alone. As I eyed the pile of clothes, I could see the gleam of gold and silk embroidery on it ... Beside them lay a good big basket that had hints about it of cold pie and wine: a half-dozen of young women stood by watching the work or the workers, both of which were worth watching, for the latter smote great strokes and were very deft in their labour, and as handsome clean-built fellows as you might find a dozen of in a summer day. They were laughing and

talking merrily with each other and the women ...

Dick looked back over his shoulder at them and said:

'They are in luck today: it's right down good sport trying to see how much pick-work one can get into an hour; and I can see those neighbours know their business well. It is not a mere matter of strength getting on quickly with such work; is it, guest?'

'I should think not,' said I, 'but to tell you the truth, I have never tried my hand at it.'

'Really?' said he gravely, 'that seems a pity; it is good work for hardening the muscles and I like it; though I admit it is pleasanter the second week than the first. Not that I am a good hand at it: the fellows used to chaff me at one [boatman's] job where I was working, I remember, and sing out to me, 'Well rowed, stroke!' 'Put your back into it, bow!'

'Not much of a joke,' quoth I.

'Well,' said Dick, 'everything seems like a joke when we have a pleasant spell of work on, and good fellows merry about us; we feel so happy, you know.' Again I pondered silently.[97]

News From Nowhere is a charming romantic fantasy (and as such is still well worth reading), but as a blueprint for a hoped-for future it has been cruelly let down by the twentieth century. Morris's socialist commonwealth, where overcrowding and overwork are banished and humanity is free to pursue artistic and social inclinations, reads as hopelessly idealistic today as it must have done for his contemporaries in the dreary factories and grimy villas of nineteenth-century London.

Voltaire
(François Marie Arouet, 1694-1778)

Voltaire, the son of a lawyer and educated by the Jesuits, early demonstrated an uncomfortably analytical mind and a freethinking approach to religion and philosophy. In the oppressive and corrupt society of eighteenth-century France's ancien régime there were many opportunities for Voltaire to protest, and many ways for him to be punished, culminating in a three-year exile in England that brought him into contact with many leading British intellects. In *Candide, or The Optimist*, he contrasts philosophical optimism with the harsh realities of human suffering. Critical of corruption in State and Church, scathing in his depiction of vain optimism, in Candide Voltaire nevertherless offers hope; that though absolute truth is beyond human grasp, it is still possible for human beings to take their destinies into their own hands and in the area of life that they have been placed, to be happy and create a peaceful society. In this hopeful scenario, according to Voltaire, human labour plays an important, almost redemptive, role.

'Human grandeur,' said Pangloss, 'is very dangerous, if we believe the testimonies of almost all philosophers ...'

'Neither need you tell me,' said Candide, 'that we must take care of our garden.'

'You are in the right,' said Pangloss; 'for when man was put into the Garden of Eden, it was with an intent to dress it: and this proves that man was not born to be idle.'

'Work then without disputing,' said Martin; 'it is the only way to render life supportable.'

The little society, one and all, entered into this laudable design; and set themselves to exert their different talents. The little piece of ground yielded them a plentiful crop.

Cunegund indeed was very ugly, but she became an excellent hand at pastry-work; Pacquet embroidered; the old woman had the care of the linen. There was none, down to Brother Giroflée, but did some service; he was a very good carpenter, and became an honest man. Pangloss used now and then to say to Candide:

'There is a concatenation of all events in the best of all possible worlds; for, in short, had you not been kicked out of a fine castle by the backside for the love of Miss Cunegund, had you not been put into the Inquisition, had you not travelled over America on foot, had you not run the Baron through the body, and had you not lost all your sheep which you brought from the good country of El Dorado, you would not have been here to eat preserved citrons and pistachio-nuts.'

'Excellently observed,' answered Candide; 'but let us take care of our garden.' [98]

G.K. Chesterton (1874-1936)

In the quotations above, the relationship between hope and faith is easy to see. A hope without foundation can become a groundless optimism that insists on hoping vainly for the best despite all the odds.

It's the need for a foundation that G.K. Chesterton underlines in his long poem 'The Ballad of the White Horse', describing King Alfred's battle against the Danes, building his portrait of Alfred's refusal to give up hope upon Alfred's vision of an encounter with the Virgin Mary, who says,

> I tell you naught for your comfort,
> Yea, naught for your desire,
> Save that the sky grows darker yet
> And the sea rises higher.

> Night shall be thrice night over you,
> And heaven an iron cope.
> Do you have joy without a cause,
> Yea, faith without a hope?

During the Second World War *The Times* once printed these two stanzas, without further explanation, as its leading article for the day.[99]

In Chesterton's poem they provide the dynamic that takes Alfred through the struggles that lie ahead, and he frequently quotes them to his attackers. Here, a 'conquered king', disguised in the Danish camp, he speaks to them with firm assurance and hope, in a resonant passage that I highly recommend for reciting at the top of your voice on solitary country walks:

> I will even answer the mighty earl
> That asked of Wessex men
> Why they be meek and monkish folk,
> And bow to the White Lord's broken yoke;
> What sign have we save blood and smoke?
> Here is my answer then.
>
> That on you is fallen the shadow,
> And not upon the Name;
> That though we scatter and though we fly
> And you hang over us like the sky,
> You are more tired of victory
> Than we are tired of shame.
>
> That though you hunt the Christian man
> Like a hare on the hill-side,
> The hare has still more heart to run
> Than you have heart to ride.

That though all lances split on you,
All swords be heaved in vain,
We have more lust again to lose
Than you to win again.

Your lord sits high in the saddle,
A broken-hearted king,
But our king Alfred, lost from fame,
Fallen among foes or bonds of shame,
In I know not what mean trade or name,
Has still some song to sing....[100]

Henry Wadsworth Longfellow (1807-1882)

The Times was not alone in gauging the power of inspirational verse to encourage hope in times of trial. Winston Churchill was fond of quoting favourite passages of verse in his war-time speeches, and brought great oratorical skill to their delivery; among those he quoted were the following from Longfellow's 'The Building of the Ship':

Sail on, O Ship of State!
Sail on, O Union, strong and great!
Humanity, with all its fears,
With all the hopes of future years,
Is hanging breathless on thy fate![101]

Arthur Hugh Clough (1819-1861)

Churchill also quoted, to immense effect, during the darkest hours of the war, a poem by Arthur Clough which urges faith and hope in equal measure:

Say not the struggle naught availeth
    The labour and the wounds are vain,

111

The enemy faints not, nor faileth,
  And as things have been they remain.
If hopes were dupes, fears may be liars;
  It may be, in yon smoke conceal'd,
Your comrades chase e'en now the fliers,
  And, but for you, possess the field.

For while the tired waves, vainly breaking,
  Seem here no painful inch to gain,
Far back, through creeks and inlets making,
  Comes silent, flooding in, the main.

And not by eastern windows only,
  When daylight comes, comes in the light;
In front the sun climbs slow, how slowly!
  But westward, look, the land is bright![102]

Hilaire Belloc (1870-1953)

Thus far we have thought of hope on the grand scale –
hope for the future of nations, hope for the future of
humankind. But the virtue of hope embraces more than
the great expectations. It is a virtue of quiet confidence, of
a prevailing intelligent optimism that has much more
content than simply hoping for the best, for it is linked
inextricably to the virtue of faith. In fact those whose faith
is firmest have the most relaxed hope, and being sure of
their future reward are not afraid sometimes to joke about
it. Hilaire Belloc, an author with a great respect for
ecclesiastical authority and the hallowed traditions of the
Church, was nevertheless fond of producing throwaway
squibs like the following:

When I shall die,
    I hope it may be said –
'His sins were scarlet
    but his books were read ...'

Adrian Plass (b. 1948)

Adrian Plass's reputation as a Christian humorist was launched when his popular magazine columns *The Sacred Diary of Adrian Plass* were published in book form. Plass has the same affectionate wit as the American humorist Garrison Keillor, and the same kindly but sharply observed view of his small-town church community. Though most of his writing is prose, he has published many poems. He is well known for his summing-up of his faith: 'God is nice, and he likes me.' Plass writes from a faith that is comfortable with itself, that can have fun with the most profound hopes of the gospel, and combines reverence, awe and a capacity for a witty rhyme.

Not a bad point at which to move on from the Christian virtue of hope. Here is Adrian Plass's 'Playground'. It will enhance your reading if you know that Adrian Plass is a very tall, very large man.

O God, I'm not anxious to snuff it,
But when the grim reaper reaps me,
I'll try to rely on my vision of Zion
I know how I want it to be.
As soon as you greet me in Heaven,
And ask what I'd like, I shall say,
'I just want a chance for my spirits to dance,
I want to be able to play.'

Tell the angels to build a soft playground,
Designed and equipped just for me,
With a vertical slide that's abnormally wide,
And oceans of green PVC.
There'll be reinforced netting to climb on,
And rubberised floors that will bend,
And no-one can die, so I needn't be shy,
If I'm tempted to land on a friend.

113

I'll go mad in the soft, squashy mangle,
And barmy with balls in the swamp,
Coloured and spherical – I'll be hysterical,
I'll have a heavenly romp.
There'll be cushions and punchbags and tyres,
In purple and yellow and red,
And a mushroomy thing that will suddenly sing,
When I kick it or sit on its head.

There'll be fountains of squash and Ribena,
to feed my continual thirst,
And none of that stuff about, 'You've had enough',
Surely heavenly bladders won't burst.
I might be too tall for the entrance,
But Lord, throw the rules in the bin,
If I am too large, tell the angel in charge
To let me bow down and come in.[103]

Charity (Love)

The word 'love' has a multitude of meanings. A chief Christian virtue, it is certainly not the sole prerogative of Christians. The medieval theologian who taught that love cannot be synthesised or acquired without God's initiative would also have been the first to point out that as all human beings bear God's image, and God is perfect love, every human being is capable of practising and recognising love. Whether he or she will actually do so, of course, is where God's initiative (the theologian would explain) comes in.

Indeed the shortage of mutual love between human beings in the world has prompted many wry observations.

Sir Walter A. Raleigh (1861-1922)

> I wish I loved the Human Race;
> I wish I loved its silly face;
> I wish I like the way it walks;
> I wish I liked the way it talks;
> And when I'm introduced to one
> I wish I thought *What Jolly Fun!*[104]

Anon.

And here are three from that versatile and prolific author, A. Nonymous:

> I love humanity, it's people I can't stand ...

> You only have to love your neighbours, you don't have to like them.

> I love the human race. All my family belong to it; and some of my wife's family, too.

The word 'charity' that has entered the English language in the company of 'faith' and 'hope' is the Authorised Version's translation of the Greek word *agapé*. In modern versions of the Bible it is usually translated 'love'. The author Hilaire Belloc (a close friend of, and collaborator with, G.K. Chesterton), in his moving essay entitled 'The Good Woman', retains the old word but fills it with many meanings.

Hilaire Belloc (1870-1953)

Strength, sustenance, and a sacramental justice are permanent in such lives, and such lives also attain before their close to so general a survey of the world that their appreciations are at once accurate and universal.

On this account she did not fail in any human conversation, nor was she ever for a moment less than herself; but always and throughout her moods her laughter was unexpected and full, her fear natural, her indignation glorious.

Above all, her charity extended like a breeze: it enveloped everything she knew. The sense of destiny faded from me as the warmth of that charity fell upon my soul; the foreknowledge of death retreated, as did every other unworthy panic.

She drew the objects of her friendship into something new; they breathed an air from another country, so that those whom she deigned to regard were, compared with other men, like the living compared with the dead; or, better still, they were like men awake while the rest were tortured by dreams and haunted of the unreal. Indeed, she had a word given to her which saved all the souls of her acquaintance.

It is not true that influence of this sort decays or

even passes into vaguer and vaguer depths of memory. It does not dissipate. It is not dissolved. It does not only spread and broaden: it also increases with the passage of time. The musicians bequeath their spirit, notably those who have loved delightful themes and easy melodies. The poets are read for ever; but those who resemble her do more, for they grow out upon the centuries – they themselves and not their arts continue. There is stuff in their legend. They are a tangible inheritance for the hurrying generations of men.

She was of this kind. She was certainly of this kind. She died upon this day in the year 1892. In these lines I perpetuate her memory. [105]

Such a passage shows that all-embracing, charitable love draws on many aspects of human character and human relationships; and to single out just one to the exclusion of all other meanings is not an adequate definition of what love is.

W. H. Auden (1907-1973)

For example love can be defined as cosmic, all-consuming, cataclysmic obsessive mutual commitment. This is *liebestod*, death-as-love, the love of Tristan and Isolde. It is the love of which W. H. Auden writes in a poem that has become well known by its use in the film *Four Weddings and a Funeral*; a love so consuming that it seems doomed to end in death, and when the loved one dies, the world comes to an end.

> Pour away the ocean and sweep up the wood;
> For nothing now can ever come to any good. [106]

All you need is love

Love can be seen also as the feelings and emotions and wonder of young love, expressed in a million lyric poems. The most-used word in popular music, and stock in trade of lyric poets, 'love' was the mainspring of the great outpouring of the 'swinging sixties', a youth revolution that broke all the rules yet fed on the same themes that have fascinated poets and musicians for centuries. Poets such as the Liverpool Poets (Adrian Henri, Roger McGough and Brian Patten) clothed the old themes in new, urban metaphor and reached people who would never have opened a poetry book before; musicians like the Beatles wrote music that inspired the young and is still played on their record players now they are mostly grown up with mortgages.

Though there was a lot of common sense spoken and sing in the subject, much else was a romantic ideal, not a practicality. 'Love me do', sang the Beatles, as if that solved everything; others like Bob Dylan were closer to the reality, though in their own work the Beatles went on to provide their own counter-balance: 'Eleanor Rigby' was a portrait of unloved loneliness seen all too frequently in those who were no longer young and were not beautiful people.

As the 1970s began, a hugely successful film cast a backward look at a world that never had been quite as innocent as the media painted it. Love, declared the 1970 film *Love Story*, means never having to say you're sorry.

Here are a few sixties voices speaking about love.

> ... Do they know they're old,
> These two who are my father and my mother
> Whose fire, from which I came, has now grown cold?

> *Elizabeth Jennings (b. 1926)*
> *'One Flesh', in* New Poems 1961 *(P.E.N anthology)*

'I got you babe'

Sonny and Cher, 1965 song title

We are like two animals escaping to dark warm holes and live our pains alone.

Jack Kerouac (1922-1969)
The Subterraneans (1960)

'Money can't buy me love'

The Beatles
1964 song title

Every woman has built into her cells and tissues the longing for a hero, sage-mythic male, to open up and share her own divinity ... Compulsive body grabbing, however, is rarely the vehicle of such communication.

Dr Timothy Leary
The Politics of Ecstasy *(1965)*

The more I revolt, the more I make love.

Wall graffiti,
quoted in Richard Neville, Playpower *(1970)*

Love is clearly a more complicated matter in reality than in the uncomplicated world of popular music, though it is such a primary force and its satisfaction such an overwhelming gratification that it is often thought to be the ultimate panacea for the world's ills. John Lennon's anthem, 'All you need is love', was written in the context of the Beatles' romantic quest for Pepperland, a dream of romantic empowerment to be shattered later in the bleaker world of post-Beatles personality conflicts and some problems for which it seemed that even love was not an all-sufficient answer: 'The Dream is Over' replaced the earlier hymns to love. Which was only a repeat of the earlier example briefly mentioned by C.S. Lewis in his important little book on love, *The Four Loves:*

> William Morris wrote a poem called *Love is enough* and someone is said to have reviewed it briefly in the words 'It isn't.' [107]

Mervyn Peake (1911-1968)

For many people today love is almost the same as lust; reduced to a dimension of sexual attraction, it is easily satisfied and easily disappointed. In a society in which youthful good looks are revered, it's possible to become too old to love. In Mervyn Peake's novel *Titus Groan* (the first of his huge *Gormenghast* trilogy), he creates a race of people called the Dwellers. The women of the Dwellers are doomed to a premature ageing:

> After they had come to their physical maturity of form their loveliness crumbled away and they became withered as flowers after their few fresh hours of brilliance and strength.
>
> No one looked middle aged. The mothers were, save for the few who had borne their children in their late teens, as ancient in appearance as their own parents.
>
> And yet they did not die as might be imagined, any earlier than is normal. On the contrary, from the long line of ancient faces at the three tables nearest the great wall, it might be imagined that their longevity was abnormal.
>
> Only their children's eyes had radiance ... Even this unnatural emanation died in these youths and girls when they had reached their nineteenth year; along with the beauty of their features, this radiance vanished too.[108]

Against the backdrop of this doomed beauty Peake tells the story of Keda, a beautiful girl of the Dwellers, over whom two men fight, for love of her, in a tragic duel:

> As he struck he withdrew the dagger, and as Rantel sank to the ground Braigon flung his weapon away .... She saw Rantel raise himself on his left arm. He groped for his dagger and felt it beside him in the dew. His life was pouring from the wound in his breast, Keda watched him as, summoning into his right arm what strength remained in his whole body, he sent the dagger running through the air with a sudden awkward movement of his arm. It found its mark in a statue's throat. Braigon's arms fell to his sides like dead weights. He tottered forward, swayed for a little, the bone hilt at his gullet, and then collapsed lifeless across the body of his destroyer.[109]

Both the men who fought for Keda's beauty lie dead; and now she grows old.

> The age that was her heritage and the inexorable fate of the Dwellers had already begun to ravage her head, a despoliation which had begun before the birth of her first child who was buried beyond the great wall, and her face had now lost all but the shadow of her beauty.[110]

Sister Wendy Beckett (b. 1930)

It's a very twentieth-century view of love. Today's media and entertainment business often portray love as the exclusive preserve of the beautiful young – as if, once youth and looks have faded, one ought not to expect to love or be loved to the same degree or depth. Read the majority of titles in the pop charts and make your own anthology!

But love as a virtue operates on a deeper level. Sister Wendy Beckett, in one of her perceptive comments about art, proposes a different view of love, one that outlives youth and sexual magnetism, as she discusses 'The Bath', a painting by Pierre Bonnard:

> If love cannot be killed, neither can it be diminished. Whatever the changes in the loved one, true love stays firm. It will deepen, but not lessen. Bonnard began to live with Marthe, later his wife, when both were young. As they aged, Marthe became progressively neurotic, spending hours each day in the bathtub. He painted her there, year after year, never seeing her as ageing or in any way different from the slender girl of his first affections. It is not Marthe herself he paints, wrinkled and exasperating, but her spirit, the perpetual beauty of what she essentially is to him, radiant in the clear water, rainbowed in the light. This is how it felt to love Marthe, how all love that is genuine feels. There is no art without love.[111]

Jack Clemo (1916-1994)

That kind of distinction underpins the work of the blind and deaf poet, Jack Clemo. A Christian whose views mellowed from the early harsh Calvinism of his first collections – a Calvinism that led him to celebrate industrialised landscapes because they obliterated fallen nature, and to reject what he called the 'lush eroticism' celebrated by so many of his fellow poets. Looking back on his solitary and tenacious path to sexual and emotional happiness, he wrote this:

> By the time I was thirty I had come to definite conclusions. I was willing to break all the rules of etiquette that had ever been invented by a stuffy and unimaginative society, but I knew that a healthy

outlook, free from cynicism, futility and world-wearisome, depended on obedience to the basic moral laws of the New Testament. I saw the silliness and sophistry of claiming that the artist, being 'creative', is under no obligation to exercise the moral discipline that would be praiseworthy in a bank clerk or a bus-driver ... If an artist cannot produce a masterpiece without seducing a child or corrupting another man's wife, then the world is better off without the masterpiece. The inviolate mystery of childhood and womanhood is more important than a word-pattern or paint-pattern that critics can call exquisite. Harriet Shelley's cry of despair as she drowned herself makes Shelley's exquisite lines about a love which 'the heavens reject not' sound hollow in their pagan hypocrisy. Browning recognised this principle: he withdrew his early admiration of Shelley on learning that the poet had been deliberately cruel to the poor child who had trustfully married him.[112]

Mother Teresa of Calcutta (1912-1997)

Love takes responsibility for the person loved: often love involves sacrifice and is costly. The work of Mother Teresa and her sisters – who staff a world-wide charitable movement for the relief of the poor, the sick and the dying – is one of the most powerful demonstrations of love in action.

> The biggest disease today is not leprosy or tuberculosis, but rather the feeling of being unwanted, uncared for and deserted by everybody. The greatest evil is the lack of love and charity, the terrible indifference towards one's neighbour who lives at the roadside assaulted by exploitation, corruption, poverty and disease.[113]

How does one practise love? Mother Teresa wrote the following to the sisters of her order:

First Friday in June 1961

My dearest Sisters,

Do not imagine that love to be true must be extraordinary. No, what we need in our love is the continuity to love the One we love. See how a lamp burns, by the continual consumption of the little drops of oil. If there are no more of these drops in the lamp, there will be no light, and the Bridegroom has a right to say: 'I do not know you.'

My children, what are these drops of oil in our lamps? They are the little things of everyday life: fidelity, punctuality, little words of kindness, just a little thought for others, those little acts of silence, of look and thought, of word and deed. These are the very drops of love that make our religious life burn with so much light.

Do not search for Jesus in far off lands; He is not there. He is in you. Just keep the lamp burning and you will always see Him.[114]

The Books of Moses

The love to which Mother Teresa directed her readers is the source of the virtue, love, drawing together the many meanings and associations of that usage; the lamp that gives the light that is to be passed on, the source of the virtue that cannot be cultivated scientifically but must come as a gift.

Hope and faith look towards their source, which is love. And Love Himself, as Moses reminded his people on the verge of the Promised Land, is gratuitous, freely given, unconditional – and costly, making demands on both parties.

The LORD did not set his affection on you and choose

you because you were more numerous than other peoples, for you were the fewest of all peoples. But it was because the LORD loved you and kept the oath he swore to your forefathers that he brought you out with a mighty hand and redeemed you from the land of slavery, from the power of Pharaoh king of Egypt. Know therefore that the LORD your God is God; he is the faithful God, keeping his covenant of love to a thousand generations of those who love him and keep his commands. But those who hate him he will repay to their face by destruction; he will not be slow to repay to their face those who hate him. Therefore, take care to follow the commands, decrees and laws I give you today.

If you pay attention to these laws and are careful to follow them, then the LORD your God will keep his covenant of love with you, as he swore to your forefathers. He will love you and bless you and increase your numbers. He will bless the fruit of your womb, the crops of your land—your grain, new wine and oil—the calves of your herds and the lambs of your flocks in the land that he swore to your forefathers to give you. You will be blessed more than any other people; none of your men or women will be childless, nor any of your livestock without young. The LORD will keep you free from every disease... [115]

George Herbert (1593-1633)

The poet George Herbert summed the matter up, in the following words of a penitent sinner exposed to the source of love and resisting that first demand of all: willingness to be loved.

Love bade me welcome: yet my soul drew back,
　　　　Guilty of dust and sin.
But quick-eyed Love, observing me grow slack
　　　　From my first entrance in,
Drew nearer to me, sweetly questioning,
　　　　If I lacked anything.

A guest, I answered, worthy to be here:
　　　　Love said, you shall be he.
I the unkind, ungrateful? Ah my dear,
　　　　I cannot look on thee.
Love took my hand, and smiling did reply,
　　　　Who made the eyes but I?
Truth Lord, but I have marred them: let my shame
　　　　Go where it doth deserve.
And know you not, says Love, who bore the blame?
　　　　My dear, then I will serve.
You must sit down, says Love, and taste my meat:
　　　　So I did sit and eat.[116]

The Moral Virtues

The remaining four virtues are known as the 'ethical', 'moral' or 'Platonic' (because that is how Plato described them) virtues. The poet William Blake (whose highly individual views on vice and virtue we have already seen) regarded them as so different to the 'theological virtues' that he said they were part of the Moral Code, a false standard ignored by Jesus who instead preached forgiveness.

Though one might quarrel with his assessment of the moral virtues taken at face value (nothing in the Bible suggests that Jesus considered justice and temperance false standards), it's right to make a distinction between the first three and the last four of the seven cardinal virtues. Where the first three are directly taken from the Bible, the last four were adapted from the virtues of the ancient world – in fact the word 'virtue' comes originally from the Latin word *vir*, meaning 'man, manly', though the term has long had a less gender-orientated meaning. A key discussion of the four moral virtues in antiquity is to be found in the fourth book of Plato's *Republic*. In Plato's ideal society, both state and individuals would be characterised by the four moral virtues. Here is Plato discussing the complex relationship between justice and temperance.

Plato (c. 428-347 BC)

And in reality justice was such as we were describing, being concerned however, not with a man's external affairs, but with an inner relationship in which he himself is more truly concerned; for the just man does not permit the several elements within him to interfere with one another, or any of them to do the work of others – he sets in order his own inner life,

and is his own master and his own law, and at peace
with himself; and when he has bound together the
three principles within him, which may be compared
to the higher, lower and middle notes of the scale, and
any that are intermediate between them – when he
has bound all these together, and is no longer many,
but has become one entirely temperate and perfectly
adjusted nature, then he proceeds to act, if he has to
act, whether in a matter of property, or in the
treatment of the body, or in some affair of politics or
private business; always thinking and calling that
which preserves and co-operates with this
harmonious condition, just and good action, and the
knowledge which presides over it, wisdom, and that
which at any time impairs this condition, he will call
unjust action, and the opinion which presides over it,
ignorance.[117]

'Virtue' in traditional Christian thought, as in classical
literature, means 'excellence'. A virtue is a mark of
maturity. The term 'cardinal virtues' recognises that there
are many virtues mentioned in the Bible – obedience (1
Peter 1:2), purity (2 Corinthians 6:6) and hospitality
(Romans 12:13) to name but three. The fact that some of
the passages that follow might illustrate more virtues than
the one under whose name they appear only goes to show
how inter-related the virtues are.

The word has often been used in a way that suggests that
virtue is a mark of super-heroes or super-saints. But though
throughout history 'ordinary' people have become known
for the remarkable qualities of virtue they possessed;
Christianity requires all Christians to strive to acquire and
develop the virtues. And as virtue is not merely a matter of
how you go about your daily life, but invokes a world-view
and a social dimension, it can lead to great things.

The implications of the virtues for pastoral work are enormous. As an ethicist, the pastor is more than an exhorter of the congregation to good 'behaviour', more than an adviser in situations of ethical crisis, and more than a facilitator of social service projects or structural social change. He or she is a spiritual guide, a shaper of personalities, a nurturer of hearts, a therapist of souls in the interest of God's kingdom. An understanding of the Christian virtues is vital for the pastor's ability to minister. Alongside close study of [New] T[estament] psychology (i.e. spirituality), the pastor's preaching and counselling ministry will relate personal needs to the growth of Christian virtues. He or she needs to be well acquainted with the spiritual disciplines and congregational activities by which the Christian virtues are cultivated. To this end he or she is aided by the classic Christian writings on the virtues, and on the lives of Christian saints.[118]

Prudence, or Wisdom

Anthony Trollope (1815-1883)

The old word for wisdom was prudence, which has
acquired the specific connotation of careful management
of one's resources both spiritual and material. Prudence in
this limited sense is certainly a moral virtue, though it is
one that, overdone, can easily become a vice. Anthony
Trollope is not so universally well known as his
contemporary Charles Dickens, but he shares Dickens's
skill at creating memorable characters. One of his finest
creations is Mrs Mason, whose frugal hospitality and utter
paranoia at the thought of any food leaving her kitchen
often drive her husband to furious despair. Here the
Masons are entertaining the attorney Mr Dockwrath and
his daughters to what Mrs Mason optimistically calls 'a hot
luncheon'.

> The covers were removed ... On the dish before the
> master of the house – a large dish which I fancy must
> have been selected by the cook with some similar
> sarcasm – there reposed three scraps, as to the nature
> of which Mr. Dockwrath, though he looked hard at
> them, was unable to enlighten himself. But Mr.
> Mason knew them well, as he now placed his eyes on
> them for the third time. They were old enemies of his,
> and his brow again became black as he looked at
> them. The scraps in fact consisted of two drumsticks
> of a fowl and some indescribable bone out of the back
> of the same ... Then, on a dish before the lady, there
> were three other morsels, black-looking and very
> suspicious to the eye, which in the course of
> conversation were proclaimed to be ham – broiled
> ham. Mrs. Mason would never allow a ham in its

proper shape to come into the room, because it is an article upon which the guests are themselves supposed to operate with the carving-knife. Lastly, on the dish before Miss Creusa there reposed three potatoes.

The face of Mr. Mason became very black as he looked at the banquet which was spread across his board, and Mrs. Mason, eyeing him across the table, saw that it was so ... the lady smiled and tried to look self-satisfied as she invited her guests to eat. 'This is ham,' said she with a little simper, 'broiled ham, Mr. Dockwrath; and there is chicken at the other end; I think they call it – devilled.'

'Shall I assist the young ladies to anything first?' said the attorney, wishing to be polite.

'Nothing, thank you,' said Miss Penelope, with a very stiff bow ...

'My daughters only eat bread and butter in the middle of the day,' said the lady. 'Creusa, my dear, will you give Mr. Dockwrath a potato. Mr. Mason, Mr. Dockwrath will probably take a bit of that chicken.'

'I would recommend him to follow the girls' example and confine himself to the bread and butter,' said the master of the house, pushing about the scraps with his knife and fork. 'There is nothing here for him to eat ... What is it you pretend to have in that dish?'

'Broiled ham. Mr. Mason.'

'Then let the ham be brought in,' said he. 'Diana, ring the bell.'

'But the ham is not cooked, Mr. Mason,' said the lady. 'Broiled ham is always better when it has not been first boiled.'

'Is there no cold meat in the house?' he asked.

'I am afraid not,' she replied ... 'You never like large joints yourself, Mr. Mason; and for ourselves we don't eat meat at luncheon.'

'Nor anybody else either, here,' said Mr. Mason in his anger ...[119]

The Book of Proverbs

Despite the truly dreadful example of Mrs Mason, there does seem to be a large element of prudence in the 'ideal woman'. On examination that ideal turns out to be not the caricature of efficient domesticity and womanly common sense that has often been used in the past to commend prudent women, but a daunting compendium of all the virtues, as can be seen in the portrait that is painted in chapter 31 of the Book of Proverbs:

A wife of noble character who can find?
　　She is worth far more than rubies.
Her husband has full confidence in her
　　and lacks nothing of value.
She brings him good, not harm,
　　all the days of her life.
She selects wool and flax
　　and works with eager hands.
She is like the merchant ships,
　　bringing her food from afar.
She gets up while it is still dark;
　　she provides food for her family
　　and portions for her servant girls.
She considers a field and buys it;
　　out of her earnings she plants a vineyard.
She sets about her work vigorously;
　　her arms are strong for her tasks.
She sees that her trading is profitable,
　　and her lamp does not go out at night.
In her hand she holds the distaff
　　and grasps the spindle with her fingers.
She opens her arms to the poor
　　and extends her hands to the needy.

132

When it snows, she has no fear for
    her household;
        for all of them are clothed in scarlet.
She makes coverings for her bed;
        she is clothed in fine linen and purple.
Her husband is respected at the city gate,
        where he takes his seat among the elders
            of the land.
She makes linen garments and sells them,
        and supplies the merchants with sashes.
She is clothed with strength and dignity;
        she can laugh at the days to come.
She speaks with wisdom,
        and faithful instruction is on her tongue.
She watches over the affairs of her household
        and does not eat the bread of idleness.
Her children arise and call her blessed;
        her husband also, and he praises her:
'Many women do noble things,
        but you surpass them all.'
Charm is deceptive, and beauty is fleeting;
        but a woman who fears the LORD
            is to be praised.
Give her the reward she has earned,
        and let her works bring her praise
            at the city gate.[120]

Charles Dickens (1812-1870)

But prudence in the sense of wise use of resources is only a small part of the virtue of wisdom. Wisdom, in the Bible, is not a matter of merely knowing things. Here is school-master Mr Gradgrind, from Charles Dickens's gallery of fictional characters, methodically rooting out wisdom in his young charges and replacing it with knowledge:

'Girl number twenty,' said Mr Gradgrind, squarely pointing with his square forefinger. 'I don't know that girl. Who is that girl?'

'Sissy Jupe, sir,' explained number twenty, blushing, standing up, and curtseying.

'Sissy is not a name,' said Mr Gradgrind. 'Don't call yourself Sissy. Call yourself Cecilia.'

'It's father as calls me Sissy, sir,' returned the young girl in a trembling voice, and with another curtsey.

'Then he has no business to do it,' said Mr Gradgrind. 'Tell him he mustn't. Cecilia Jupe. Let me see. What is your father?'

'He belongs to the horse-riding, if you please, sir.' ...

'Give me your definition of a horse.'

(Sissy Jupe thrown into the greatest alarm by this command.)

'Girl number twenty unable to define a horse!' said Mr Gradgrind, for the general behoof of all the little pitchers. 'Girl number twenty possessed of no facts, in reference to one of the commonest of animals! Some boy's definition of a horse. Bitzer, yours.'

The square finger, moving here and there, lighted suddenly on Bitzer, perhaps because he chanced to sit in the same ray of sunshine which, darting in at one of the bare windows of the intensely whitewashed room, irradiated Sissy. For, the boys and girls sat on the face of the inclined plane in two compact bodies, divided up the centre by a narrow interval; and Sissy, being at the corner of a row on the sunny side, came in for the beginning of a sunbeam, of which Bitzer, being at the corner of a row on the other side, a few rows in advance, caught the end. But, whereas the girl was so dark-eyed and dark-haired, that she seemed to receive a deeper and more lustrous colour from the sun, when it shone upon her, the boy was so light-eyed and light-haired that the self-same rays

appeared to draw out of him what little colour he ever
possessed. His cold eyes would hardly have been eyes,
but for the short ends of lashes which, by bringing
them into immediate contrast with something paler
than themselves, expressed their form. His short-
cropped hair might have been a mere continuation of
the sandy freckles on his forehead and face. His skin
was so unwholesomely deficient in the natural tinge,
that he looked as though, if he were cut, he would
bleed white.

'Bitzer,' said Thomas Gradgrind, 'Your definition of
a horse.'

'Quadruped. Graminivorous. Forty teeth, namely
twenty-four grinders, four eye-teeth, and twelve
incisive. Sheds coat in the spring; in marshy
countries, sheds hoofs, too. Hoofs hard, but requiring
to be shod with iron. Age known by marks in mouth.'
Thus (and much more) Bitzer.

'Now girl number twenty,' said Mr Gradgrind. 'You
know what a horse is.' [121]

Facts, facts and more facts is Thomas Gradgrind's recipe,
but wisdom is a different matter. It means having the
proper perspective on things.

C.S. Lewis (1898-1963)

Even the science of material objects changes when
perception changes: 'The eye altering alters all,' as Blake
observed.[122] And it was a hard lesson for Eustace to learn
in Narnia, as he struggled with elementary Narnian
cosmology:

'Do you mean you were flying in the air?' Eustace
blurted out.

'I was a long way above the air, my son,' replied the
Old Man. 'I am Ramandu. But I see you stare at one

another and have not heard of this name. And no wonder, for the days when I was a star had ceased long before any of you knew this world, and all the constellations have changed.'

'Golly,' said Edmund under his breath. 'He's a *retired* star.'

'Aren't you a star any longer?' asked Lucy.

'I am a star at rest, my daughter,' answered Raman-du. 'When I set for the last time, decrepit and old beyond all that you can reckon, I was carried to this island. I am not so old as I was then. Every morning a bird brings me a fire-berry from the valleys in the Sun, and each fire-berry takes away a little of my age. And when I have become as young as the child that was born yesterday, then I shall take my rising again (for we are at earth's eastern rim) and once more tread the great dance.'

'In our world,' said Eustace, 'a star is a huge ball of flaming gas.'

'Even in your world, my son, that is not what a star is but only what it is made of.' [123]

Thus 'understanding' – a word often used in this sense – does not mean a theoretical knowledge of how something works, but a grasp of how matters look from the perspective of God.

Asaph the Psalmist

In this psalm, Asaph describes the getting of wisdom; not knowledge obtained by study, but an understanding gained by shifting the place from which he was looking at his situation. When he went into the sanctuary, then he became wise.

> Surely God is good to Israel, to those who are pure in heart.

136

But as for me, my feet had almost slipped; I had nearly
     lost my foothold.
For I envied the arrogant when I saw the prosperity of
     the wicked.
They have no struggles; their bodies are healthy and
     strong.
They are free from the burdens common to man;
they are not plagued by human ills.
Therefore pride is their necklace; they clothe themselves
     with violence.
From their callous hearts comes iniquity;
the evil conceits of their minds know no limits.
They scoff, and speak with malice;
in their arrogance they threaten oppression.
Their mouths lay claim to heaven,
and their tongues take possession of the earth.
Therefore their people turn to them and drink up waters
     in abundance.
They say, 'How can God know? Does the Most High
     have knowledge?'
This is what the wicked are like – always carefree, they
     increase in wealth.
Surely in vain have I kept my heart pure;
in vain have I washed my hands in innocence.
All day long I have been plagued; I have been punished
     every morning.
If I had said, 'I will speak thus,' I would have betrayed
     your children.
When I tried to understand all this, it was oppressive to
     me
till I entered the sanctuary of God; then
     I understood their final destiny.[124]

Dietrich Bonhoeffer (1906-1945)

In 1933 Bonhoeffer, in protest at Nazi anti-Semitism, joined the Confessing Church, which resisted the Nazi policy. He spent the next two years as a pastor of German congregations in London, returning to Germany in 1935 to take up the leadership of a Confessing Church seminary in Pomerania; the seminary was eventually shut down by the authorities. When the war began, Bonhoeffer became a resistance worker against Hitler. In 1943 he was arrested attempting to smuggle seven Jews to safety and in 1945 was hanged by the Nazis for plotting against Hitler.

The meditation below, on Psalm 119, was composed in 1939-1940 during a period of relative calm and happiness in his life. Perhaps symbolically, it was never finished. It is a meditation both on the sin of pride and the virtue of wisdom; for only with godly wisdom, he writes, can one properly understand the power and plight of the proud.

Psalm 119:21 – You have rebuked the insolent; cursed are they who stray from your commandments!

God hates the insolent, those who are content with themselves, who care nothing for justice and mercy, who despise the Word of God and the faithful. Pride before God is the root of all disobedience, all violence, all irresponsibility. Pride is the root of all rebellion and destruction. Confronting all pride and insolence, however, is a fearful warning, of which the proud themselves comprehend nothing, but the faithful do; it is the Gospel. 'God opposes the proud, but gives grace to the humble.' (1 Peter 5:5) The cross of Jesus Christ, which shows that God is with the weak and the humble, is God's rebuke to the insolent. They may achieve victory over all human beings, but against God they will come to nought.

Whoever believes in the Gospel sees the Word of God hanging over the insolence of this earth. The preaching of the Word of God is the only serious rebuke to a humanity grown proud. But, along with his Word, God has also given signs of his might. In the midst of history, here and there, God's rebuke can be seen, and the community of the faithful look with shuddering and amazement at the proud, who even now in their time fall and are destroyed. They are kept from any hypocritical certainty, however, because they see that innocent people are always destroyed along with the proud; and so the visible judgements of God remain hidden and obscure even for the faithful. Only the Word remains incontrovertibly clear when it pronounces its curse on the godless: 'Cursed are they who stray from your commandments!' In the law it says: 'Cursed be he who does not confirm the words of this law by doing them.' (Deut. 27:26) Can we speak this word without being convicted by it ourselves? Is it a word only for others and not for ourselves? The curse upon the transgressors of the law of God is God's right and ...

[Here the manuscript breaks off.][125]

Justice

The most celebrated exponent of justice is probably King Solomon; and his best-known case, the dispute between the quarrelling mothers.

> Now two prostitutes came to the king and stood before him. One of them said, 'My lord, this woman and I live in the same house. I had a baby while she was there with me. The third day after my child was born, this woman also had a baby. We were alone; there was no-one in the house but the two of us. During the night this woman's son died because she lay on him. So she got up in the middle of the night and took my son from my side while I your servant was asleep. She put him by her breast and put her dead son by my breast. The next morning, I got up to nurse my son – and he was dead! But when I looked at him closely in the morning light, I saw that it wasn't the son I had borne.'
>
> The other woman said, 'No! The living one is my son; the dead one is yours.'
>
> But the first one insisted, 'No! The dead one is yours; the living one is mine.'
>
> And so they argued before the king.
>
> The king said, 'This one says, "My son is alive and your son is dead," while that one says, "No! Your son is dead and mine is alive."'
>
> Then the king said, 'Bring me a sword.'
>
> So they brought a sword for the king. He then gave an order: 'Cut the living child in two and give half to one and half to the other.'
>
> The woman whose son was alive was filled with com passion for her son and said to the king, 'Please, my lord, give her the living baby! Don't kill him!'

But the other said, 'Neither I nor you shall have him. Cut him in two!'

Then the king gave his ruling: 'Give the living baby to the first woman. Do not kill him; she is his mother.'

When all Israel heard the verdict the king had given, they held the king in awe, because they saw that he had wisdom from God to administer justice.[126]

Mark Twain
(Samuel Langhorne Clemens, 1835-1910)

When justice is called a virtue, it does not of course follow that human justice is what is being described. Human justice and judges are prone to fallibility and corruption; the only true justice in society is that which places itself under a higher justice than itself.

So argues Mark Twain in *A Connecticut Yankee at King Arthur's Court*, a wittily acerbic tale of an American at the end of the nineteenth century who is transported back into the past and King Arthur's England. Twain's often-black humour spares neither Church nor State, and as with most books of this type modern society is castigated by implication. Here is Twain at his most powerful, describing his hero as he watches a sombre procession:

> There was a cart with a coffin in it, and on the coffin sat a comely young girl of about eighteen suckling a baby, which she squeezed to her breast in a passion of love every while ... Our master secured a good place for us near the gallows. A priest ... helped the girl up, and said comforting words to her, and made the under-sheriff provide a stool for her. He began to tell the story of the case ... 'Law is intended to mete out justice. Sometimes it fails. This cannot be helped. We can only grieve, and be resigned, and pray for the soul of him who falls unfairly by the arm of the law, and

that his fellows may be few. A law sends this poor young thing to death – and it is right. But another law had placed her where she must commit her crime or starve, with her child – and before God that law is responsible for both her crime and her ignominious death! ... Little by little all her small possessions went for food. When she could no longer pay her rent, they turned her out of doors. She begged, while she had strength; when she was starving, at last, and her milk failing, she stole a piece of linen cloth of the value of a fourth part of a cent, thinking to sell it and save her child. But she was seen by the owner of the cloth .... The time is come, my child; let me pray over thee – not *for* thee, dear abused poor heart and innocent, but for them that be guilty of thy ruin and death, who need it more.'

After his prayer they put the noose round the young girl's neck ... When all was ready the priest gently pulled and tugged and forced the child out of the mother's arms ... Then she went on her knees ... 'Oh, my child, my darling, it will die! It has no home, it has no father, no mother – '

'It has them all!' said that good priest. 'All these will I be to it till I die.'

You should have seen her face then! Gratitude? Lord, what do you want with words to express that? Words are only painted fire; a look is the fire itself. She gave that look, and carried it away to the treasury of heaven, where all things that are divine belong.[127]

The parable of the unjust debtor

Twain's invocation of a law that stands above all human law, a justice that exists to confirm or deny all human justice, is based on a common theme in the Bible. Jesus made the point tellingly with the following parable.

Then Peter came to Jesus and asked, 'Lord, how many times shall I forgive my brother when he sins against me? Up to seven times?'

Jesus answered, 'I tell you, not seven times, but seventy-seven times. Therefore, the kingdom of heaven is like a king who wanted to settle accounts with his servants. As he began the settlement, a man who owed him ten thousand talents was brought to him. Since he was not able to pay, the master ordered that he and his wife and his children and all that he had be sold to repay the debt.

The servant fell on his knees before him. "Be patient with me," he begged, "and I will pay back everything." The servant's master took pity on him, cancelled the debt and let him go.

But when that servant went out, he found one of his fellow-servants who owed him a hundred denarii. He grabbed him and began to choke him. "Pay back what you owe me!" he demanded.

His fellow-servant fell to his knees and begged him, "Be patient with me, and I will pay you back."

But he refused. Instead, he went off and had the man thrown into prison until he could pay the debt. When the other servants saw what had happened, they were greatly distressed and went and told their master everything that had happened.

Then the master called the servant in. "You wicked servant," he said, "I cancelled all that debt of yours because you begged me to. Shouldn't you have had mercy on your fellow-servant just as I had on you?" In anger his master turned him over to the jailers to be tortured, until he should pay back all he owed.

This is how my heavenly Father will treat each of you unless you forgive your brother from your heart.' 128

William Shakespeare (1564-1616)

Justice is a theme that is also found several times in the works of Shakespeare, especially in those plays that portray fallible or immoral human justice. In passages like that below from *Measure for Measure*, Shakespeare reminds us that the Bible is a treatise on forgiveness from Genesis through to Revelation. The gospel's story of the human race is one of rebels needing to be pardoned and of a guiltless judge who paid the penalty himself. 'Freely you have received, freely give' (Matthew 10:8) applies as much to forgiveness as to charity. So Christians have the greatest possible reason to strive for perfect compassion and perfect justice: it is that perfect compassion and perfect justice have already been shown to them. Angelo, the Duke's deputy and thereby the administrator of justice, is left with a nice problem of relative justice.

> *Angelo:* Your brother is a forfeit of the law,
> And you but waste your words.
> *Isabella:* Alas, alas!
> Why, all the souls that were were forfeit once;
> And He that might the vantage best have took
> Found out the remedy. How would you be,
> If He, which is the top of judgement, should
> But judge you as you are? O, think on that;
> And mercy then will breathe within your lips,
> Like man new made.
> *Angelo:* Be you content, fair maid.
> It is the law, not I condemn your brother:
> Were he my kinsman, brother, or my son,
> It should be thus with him ...
> *Isabella:* ... Merciful Heaven,
> Thou rather with thy sharp and sulphurous bolt
> Split'st the unwedgeable and gnarled oak
> Than the soft myrtle: but man, proud man,

Drest in a little brief authority
Most ignorant of what he's most assured
His glassy essence, like an angry ape,
Plays such fantastic tricks before high heaven
As make the angles weep; who, with our spleens
Would all themselves laugh mortal.[129]

Martin Luther (1483-1546)

Luther, the German theologian who launched the Protestant Reformation, was a man of formidable learning and great zest and skill in debate, which in those days was often rowdy and prolonged. One of his disputes was with Desiderius Erasmus, who having at first supported the Reformation went on to become one of its strongest opponents; he was in dispute with Luther from 1524-1526.

The Bondage of the Will is Luther's response to Erasmus's *Discussion of Free Will*; a bitter debate ensued concerning the role of faith and providence in the salvation of mankind. Luther regarded *The Bondage of the Will* as his finest work, and it is a thorough summary (Erasmus called it 'a huge book') of the theology of salvation through faith that was the core of the Lutheran Reformation.

In the closing pages Luther sets the whole discussion into the context of the absolute justice of God.

> Is it not, pray, universally held to be most unjust that bad men should prosper, and good men be afflicted? Yet that is the way of the world. Hereupon some of the greatest minds have fallen into denying the existence of God, and imagining that Chance governs all things at random ... Yet all this, which looks so much like injustice in God, and is traduced as such by arguments which no reason or light of nature can resist, is most easily cleared up by the light of the gospel and the knowledge of grace, which teaches us

that though the wicked flourish in their bodies, yet they perish in their souls. And a summary explanation of this whole inexplicable problem is found in a single little word: *There is life after this life; and all that is not punished and repaid here will be punished and repaid there; for this life is nothing more than a precursor, or, rather, a beginning, of the life that is to come* ...[130]

Thomas Watson (d. 1686)

Yet justice, whether divine or human, cannot be considered separately from mercy. Thomas Watson, a seventeenth-century Puritan minister who was among the London ministers who protested against the execution of Charles I, wrote a manual of theology – described by the Victorian preacher Charles Haddon Spurgeon as 'one of the most precious of the peerless works of the Puritans' – entitled *The Body of Divinity*. He wrote the following as an involved and sometimes persecuted observer of the troubled time in which he lived.

As God's mercy makes the saints [believers] happy, so it should make them humble. Mercy is not the fruit of our goodness, but the fruit of God's goodness. Mercy is an alms that God bestows. They have no cause to be proud that live upon the alms of God's mercy. 'If I be righteous, yet will I not lift up my head,' Job x 15: all my righteousness is the effect of God's mercy, therefore I will be humble and will not lift up my head.

Mercy stays the speedy execution of God's jus-tice. Sinners continually provoke God, and make 'the fury come up in his face.' Ezek xxxviii 18. Whence is it God does not presently arrest and condemn them? It is not that God cannot do it, for he is armed with omnipotence, but it is from his mercy. Mercy gets a reprieve from the sinner, and stops the speedy process of justice. God would, by his goodness, lead sinners to repentance.[131]

Some footnotes on justice

O God, from whom all holy desires, all good counsels, and all just works do proceed; Give unto thy servants that peace which the world cannot give.

> Book of Common Prayer *(1662)*
> *Evening Prayer, Second Collect*

Immediately the freethinkers started to question if God existed, the problem of justice became the most important question of all.

> *Albert Camus (1913-1960)*
> The Rebel *(1951)*

> The Law is the true embodiment
> Of everything that's excellent.
> It has no kind of fault or flaw,
> And I, my Lords, embody the Law.

> *W.S. Gilbert (1836-1911)*
> Iolanthe *(1882)*

'Do you hear his worship ask if you've anything to say?' inquired the jailer ...

'No,' replied the Dodger, 'not here, for this ain't the shop for justice ... Ah! (to the Bench) it's no use your looking frightened; I won't show you no mercy, not a ha'porth of it. *You'll* pay for this, my fine fellers. I wouldn't be you for something! I wouldn't go free, now, if you was to fall down on your knees and ask me. Here, carry me off to prison! Take me away!'

> *Charles Dickens (1812-70)*
> Oliver Twist *(1838)*

The law is not a 'light' for you or any man to see by; the law is not an instrument of any kind. The law is a causeway upon which so long as he keeps to it a citizen may walk safely.

Words of Thomas More in
Robert Bolt (1924-1995),
A Man for all Seasons (1960)

Fortitude

Fortitude, or perseverance, or determination, or patience – this virtue combines many qualities. It is often thought of as a rather wimpish virtue; what you do when you can't make things better. Sometimes it is hardly a virtue at all, when it is forced on one by convention or upbringing; a man refraining from weeping because he has been taught that it is unmanly to weep is not necessarily, in most societies, being particularly virtuous. He may merely be proving that he has not forgotten his lessons.

Ambrose Bierce (1842-1914)

The American writer Ambrose Bierce's cynical definition, in his *Devil's Dictionary*, is typical of the way this virtue has often been disparaged.

> PATIENCE, n. A minor form of despair, disguised as a virtue.[132]

Cassian, John (c.360-435)

Let's first dispose of Ambrose Bierce's witty but false definition. Cassian was a monk who had a great influence on the later Benedictines and devoted much of his life to teaching and training monks. He was a contemporary of the Desert Fathers, in whose teachings the seven deadly sins are thought to have been first defined, and a lecturer to the leading figures in early Eastern Christian mysticism. Discussing 'true patience', Cassian gives the following example:

> A religious woman was once so ardent in pursuing patience that she sought out temptation instead of

avoiding it. She wanted to test herself and teach herself not to yield. She was of aristocratic ancestry, and lived at Alexandria, serving the Lord faithfully in the house left to her by her parents. She went to Bishop Athanasius of blessed memory, and asked him to allow her to support one of the widows at present being maintained by the Church's treasury. Her actual words were, 'Give me one of the sisters to look after.'

The bishop, concerned that the woman might live to regret her generosity, arranged for her to look after a widow known to be considerate and courteous. The woman would have none of it.

After a few days she returned to Bishop Athanasius and said: 'I asked you to give me someone to refresh, someone whom I could try to please by my services.'

[... So Athanasius] gave secret orders that she should be given the worst of the widows, the one who bawled and brawled and drank and gossiped more than any other widow guilty of these vices. It was all too easy to find the woman ... Now the only thanks [the donor] got was reviling and wrong-doing and cursing; the woman complained continually ... Her wanton abuse culminated in blows. But the lady meekly redoubled her efforts to serve her. She learnt to overcome the harridan by obeying her quietly, and to soften her abusive rage by humanity and gentleness.

By these exercises she was strengthened and obtained the true patience for which she was looking. And she went to Bishop Athanasius and thanked him for the good his selection had done to her. She said that he had (at last) given her what she wanted, a most wonderful teacher of patience, whose constant abuse, like the oil with which a man smears himself when about to wrestle, had trained her patience to be perfect. 'At last you have given me someone to look after, for the first rather honoured and refreshed me by her services.' 133

Frederic William Farrar (1831-1903)

Fortitude, in Cassian's sense of putting up with frustrations and unfairness, was stock-in-trade for the writers of moral Victorian school stories, which often featured a virtuous schoolboy accused of another's wrongdoing. He manfully bore the disgrace of the real culprit on his young shoulders until, with the last chapter looming, the culprit owned up and the rest of the school were able to blame themselves for their readiness to think badly of such a splendid young man, and could appropriately celebrate the moral virtue of the patient hero.

By far the most idealised of such portraits are to be found in the works of Frederic William Farrar, Head of Marlborough School 1871-1876 and an Anglican clergyman who rose to become Dean of Canterbury (1895-1903). He wrote the school stories *Eric, or Little by Little* (1858), *Julian Home* (1859), and *St Winifred's, or The World of School* (1862). His *Life of Christ* (1874) is the only one of his religious works still much read.

Though it is the unjustly-maligned 'plucky Walter Evson' who dominates *St Winifred's*, Farrar created in the sickly 'Dubbs' Daubeny a schoolboy of utter saintliness – and compelling implausibility.

'Let's come and see Dubbs before tea,' said Walter, on rejoining the other two. 'Henderson told me he was ill in bed, poor fellow.'

They went at once to the cottage, detached from the rest of the school buildings, to which all invalids were removed, and they were allowed to go to Daubeny's room; but, although he was expecting their visit, he had fallen asleep. They noticed a worn and weary expression upon his countenance, but it was pleasant to look at him; for although he was a very ordinary-looking boy, with somewhat heavy features, yet whatever beauty can be infused into any face by honesty of purpose and innocence of heart, was to be found in his; and you could not speak to Daubeny for five minutes without being attracted by the sense that you were talking to one whose character was singularly free from falsehood and vanity, and singularly unstained by evil thoughts.

'There lies one of the best and worthiest fellows in the school,' whispered Power, as he raised his candle to look at him.[134]

Daubeny is only one of Farrar's many schoolboys who face accusation and slander with a sweet fortitude that makes one suspect that the Dean had long forgotten that he was writing about boys in their early teens, and was now embarked on the kind of edifying Saint's Life that was standard fare in the Middle Ages.

Talbot Baines Reed (1853-1893)

The theme of manly Christian fortitude was common in Victorian school stories, though not all wrote with the stupefying dullness of Farrar. Talbot Baines Reed (1853-1893) was a prolific author of boys' school stories whose *Fifth Form at St Dominic's* (1881) is still read today. Reed, like Farrar, wants to use the novel as a vehicle for Christian preaching, but he possesses two qualities that Farrar does not; a thorough understanding of school life and interests, and the ability to tell a good story well.

The Fifth Form at St Dominic's has a gallery of well-drawn characters, and a genuinely involving plot. Oliver Greenfield takes the role of the misunderstood, falsely accused victim, bearing his undeserved disgrace with fortitude and composure. Tony Pembury, the sardonic acid-tongued classmate who observes rather more than he chooses to talk about, acts as the author's mouthpiece on several occasions; Oliver's brother Stephen, foolishly lured into a life of schoolboy crime by the school lout and wastrel Loman, repents and changes his ways, as does Loman himself who as the greater sinner pays the higher price – expulsion.

Here is the pivotal scene at the school speech day in which Oliver, suspected (wrongly) of cheating, goes up to collect from the Doctor (headmaster) and visiting nobleman the prize that his classmates think he has won by cheating.

'The next name,' says the Doctor, referring to his list, 'is that of the of the Nightingale Scholarship – (sensation) – and I may tell your lordship the boy is, in the opinion of his examiners and myself, one of the most promising boys for his age that St. Dominic's has known. The examiners report that his answers to the questions on the paper deserve the greatest credit. I will say only this before his face: Nightingale Scholarship – Greenfield senior.'

A solemn silence marks the close of the Doctor's speech, in the midst of which Oliver, with pale face, but otherwise unmoved, advances to where the noble Earl stands. A few of the strangers greet his appearance with a clapping of hands, but the sound falls strangely on the silence all around .... You might hear a pin fall as the old gentleman, in dumb show, places the certificate into the boy's hands and tries to get at the words which the silence has scared away.

Oliver waits no longer than he can help. With a bow, he takes the parchment and turns to quit the scene.

It is at this moment, that somewhere or other in

the hall, there rises a faint, almost whispered hiss. Slight as it is, it falls with startling effect upon the dead silence which reigns. Then, like the first whisper of a storm, it suddenly grows and swells and rushes, angrily and witheringly, about the head of the wretched Oliver. Then as suddenly it dies away into silence, and the presentation of the Nightingale Scholarship is at an end.

[*Later, as the term ends, Wraysford of the Fifth and Pembury are at the school gates.*] At the drive gate two boys are standing waiting for the omnibus. Wraysford and Pembury are upon them before they observe that they are Oliver and his brother.

What is to be done? There is no escaping them – they must pass; yet both of them, somehow, would at that moment – they couldn't tell why – have dropped into the earth.

Oliver looks up as they approach.

Now or never! Wraysford feels he must say something!

'Goodbye, Greenfield,' he says. 'I hope – '

Oliver quietly takes Stephen's arm and turns on his heel.

Wraysford stares after him for a moment, and then slowly goes on his way, breathing hard.

'I wonder,' said Pembury, after a long silence – 'I wonder, Wray, if it's possible we are wrong about that fellow?'

Wraysford says nothing.

'He doesn't act like a guilty person. Just fancy, Wray' – and here Tony pulls up short, in a state of perturbation – 'just fancy if you and I and the rest have been making fools of ourselves all the term!'

Ah! My Fifth Form heroes, just fancy![135]

John Bunyan (1628-1688)

The Pilgrim's Progress is a feast of virtues and vices brilliantly portrayed, and choosing from them is a difficult and highly personal task ... For fortitude, and with it courage, I have included the death of Mr Valiant-for-Truth, because too few readers who enjoy Part I of Bunyan's masterpiece go on to explore the riches of Part II; and because the passage in which the old warrior's death is described, itself part of the rising crescendo that forms the book's conclusion, is a highlight of one of the great prose masterpieces of English literature.

> After this it was noised abroad that Mr Valiant-for-Truth was taken with a summons, by the same Post as the other; and had this for a token that the summons was true, *That his pitcher was broken at the fountain.* When he understood it, he called for his friends, and told them of it. Then said he, 'I am going to my fathers, and though with great difficulty I am got hither, yet now I do not repent me of all the trouble I have been at to arrive where I am. My sword, I give to him that shall succeed me in my pilgrimage, and my courage and skill, to him that can get it. My marks and scars I carry with me, to be a witness for me that I have fought his battles who now will be my rewarder.' When the day that he must go hence was come many accompanied him to the River side, into which, as he went, he said, *'Death, where is thy sting?'* And as he went down deeper, he said, *'Grave where is thy victory?'* So he passed over, and the trumpets sounded for him on the other side.[136]

George Orwell (Eric Blair), (1903-1950)

An allegory of a different kind is Orwell's terse, brilliant attack on totalitarian governments, *Animal Farm*. One of Orwell's most effective characterisations is the doomed cart-horse Boxer, whose sweet nature and increasing patience as the situation deteriorates make him certain to be a casualty of Napoleon the pig's new régime at Animal Farm.

It was a slow, laborious process. Frequently it took a whole day of exhausting effort to drag a single boulder to the top of the quarry, and sometimes when it was pushed over the edge it failed to break. Nothing could have been achieved without Boxer, whose strength seemed equal to that of all the rest of the animals put together. When the boulder began to slip and the animals cried out in despair at finding themselves dragged down the hill, it was always Boxer who strained himself against the rope and brought the boulder to a stop. To see him toiling up the slope inch by inch, his breath coming fast, the tips of his hoofs clawing at the ground, and his great sides matted with sweat, filled everybody with admiration. Clover warned him sometimes to be careful not to overstrain himself, but Boxer would never listen to her. His two slogans, 'I will work harder' and 'Napoleon is always right', seemed to him a sufficient answer to all problems.[137]

Terry Waite (b. 1939)

John Bunyan was imprisoned for his beliefs (the experience was rather less harrowing than some of his biographers have portrayed it), and wrote his masterpiece in prison. In modern times, many prisoners of conscience have caught the imagination of millions because of the fortitude and resilience with which they endured prison and immense suffering.

In January 1987, Terry Waite, the envoy of the Archbishop of Canterbury, was captured by Hezbollah in Lebanon. He spent the next 1,763 days in captivity. In this extract from the biography that he wrote in his head during those days, and later published, he describes how he was told he had been sentenced to death and was allowed to write a single letter.

The letter seems sorely inadequate, but it's the best I can do. The man in the suit asks for it and takes it from me.

'Who are these names?'

'They are my family and friends.'

He reads the letter.

'You want eat?'

'No, thank you.'

'You want a last drink – whisky, brandy, beer?'

That is a taunt.

'I would like a cup of tea, please.'

The guard is sent into the kitchen to prepare tea. In a few moments he returns and hands me a plastic beaker. I sip the tea slowly.

'You want more?'

'No, thank you.'

'Stand.'

'I would like to say my prayers.'

'You can do that.'

I say the Lord's Prayer aloud and then silently pray for all those whom I love and also for my captors.

'You want to say anything?'

'No.' I am determined not to plead for my life in any way.

'Stand.'

I struggle to my feet. The radio is playing Arabic music. What a way to die. I feel cold metal against the side of my temple.

'You have anything to say?'

'Nothing.'

There is a silence. I wait. The gun is removed. The old man speaks. 'Not tonight – later.'

I sit down. My chains are replaced and locked. I lie down and within a few moments am asleep, utterly exhausted.[138]

Scott of the Antarctic
(Robert Falcon Scott, 1868-1912)

Terry Waite's fortitude was in the face of extreme psychological suffering. In their last expedition to the South Pole, Scott and his companions endured extreme physical suffering, and their fortitude has often been cited as a great example of Christian courage. The diaries and records of the expedition were retrieved from the polar ice when the bodies of the team were recovered; among their effects were Scott's diaries and a number of letters, including a Message to the Public, which ends as follows:

> I do not think human beings ever came through such a month as we have come through, and we should have got through in spite of the weather but for the sickening of a second companion, Captain Oates, and a shortage of fuel in our depôts for which I cannot account, and finally, but for the storm which has fallen on us within 11 miles of the depôt at which we hoped to secure our final supplies. Surely misfortune could scarcely have exceeded this last blow. We arrived within 11 miles of our old One Ton Camp with fuel for one last meal and food for two days. For four days we have been unable to leave the tent – the

gale howling about us. We are weak, writing is difficult, but for my own sake I do not regret this journey, which has shown that Englishmen can endure hardships, help one another, and meet death with as great a fortitude as ever in the past. We took risks, we knew we took them; things have come out against us, and therefore we have no cause for complaint, but bow to the will of Providence, determined still to do our best to the last. But if we have been willing to give our lives to this enterprise, which is for the honour of our country, I appeal to our countrymen to see that those who depend on us are properly cared for.

Had we lived, I should have had a tale to tell of the hardihood, endurance and courage of my companions which would have stirred the heart of every Englishman. These rough notes and our bodies must tell the tale, but surely, surely a great rich country like ours will see that those who are dependent on us are properly provided for – R. Scott.[139]

James Barrie (1860-1937)

One of Scott's farewell letters was to his friend the playwright James Barrie, author of *Peter Pan*. Barrie read extracts from the letter in an address he gave as Rector to the students of St Andrews University in 1922, later published as a book entitled *Courage*:

'We are pegging out in a very comfortless spot. Hoping this letter may be found and sent to you, I write you a word of farewell ... We are in a desperate state – feet frozen, etc., no fuel, and a long way from food, but it would do your heart good to be in our tent, to hear our songs and our cheery conversation ... We are very near the end ... We did intend to finish

159

ourselves when things proved like this, but we have decided to die naturally without.'

I think it may uplift you all to stand for a moment by that tent and listen, as he says, to their songs and cheery conversation. When I think of Scott I remember the strange Alpine story of the youth who fell down a glacier and was lost, and of how a scientific companion, one of several who accompanied him, all young, computed that the body would again appear at a certain date and place many years afterwards. When that time came round some of the survivors returned to the glacier to see if the prediction would be fulfilled; all old men now; and the body reappeared as young as on the day he left them. So Scott and his comrades emerge out of the white immensities always young.

How comely a thing is affliction borne cheerfully, which is not beyond the reach of the humblest of us. What is beauty? It is these hard-bitten men singing courage to you from their tent.[140]

Njal's Saga (c.1280)

A different kind of fortitude again is that displayed in the ancient saga of Njal, which like all the Icelandic sagas is an orally transmitted tale of pagan life eventually written down by Christian monks after the conversion of Iceland to Christianity and the arrival of writing. The story of Njal Thorgeirsson shows a society in which the ideals of paganism and Christianity coexist with raging blood feuds and cycles of vengeance, and Njal's supreme fortitude as he and his wife Bergthora meet their death by being burned alive in their home by their enemies combines the finest of pagan and Christian epic qualities. Njal's desire to break the endless revenge cycle stems from his Christian beliefs, but the pagan characters too face death in the pagan way, a smile and a quip on their lips, for it is in making a good death that they validate their bravery and claim their place in the afterlife.

Flosi went up to the door and called Njal and Bergthora over to speak to him; when they came, he said, 'I want to offer you leave to come out, for you do not deserve to burn.'

'I have no wish to go outside,' said Njal, 'for I am an old man now and ill-equipped to avenge my sons; and I do not want to live on shame.'

Flosi said to Bergthora, 'You come out, Bergthora, for under no circumstances do I want you to burn.'

Bergthora replied, 'I was given to Njal in marriage when young, and I have promised him that we would share the same fate.'

Then they both went back inside.

'What shall we do now?' asked Bergthora.

'Let us go to our bed,' said Njal, 'and lie down.'

Then Bergthora said to little Thord, Kari's son, 'You are to be taken out. You are not to burn.'

The boy replied, 'But that's not what you promised, grandfather. You said that we would never be parted; and so it shall be, for I would much prefer to die beside you both.'

She carried the boy to the bed. Njal said to his steward, 'Take not where we lay ourselves down and how we dispose ourselves, for I shall not move from here however much the smoke or flames distress me. Then you can know where to look for our remains.'

The steward said he would.

An ox had recently been slaughtered, and the hide was lying nearby. Njal told the steward to spread the hide over them, and he promised to do so.

Njal and Bergthora lay down on the bed and put the boy between them. Then they crossed themselves and the boy, and commended their souls to God. These were the last words they were heard to speak.

... Skarp-Hedin had seen his father go to lie down and the preparations he had made.

'Father is going early to bed,' he said. 'And that is only natural, for he is an old man.' [141]

Temperance

G.K. Chesterton (1874-1936)

Temperance is not abstinence. Most good things in life are enjoyable if taken in moderation, and hateful if taken to excess. Some world religions have built themselves on such principles. Christianity, perhaps, has had an ongoing problem with temperance, preferring at times an anti-worldly abstinence that the Bible never commanded. G.K. Chesterton was a robust writer on this as on many subjects, for example in his provocative essay 'Wine when it is Red'.

Let a man walk ten miles steadily on a hot summer's day along a dusty English road, and he will soon discover why beer was invented. The fact that beer has a very slight stimulating quality will be quite among the smallest reasons that induce him to ask for it. In short, he will not be in the least desiring alcohol; he will be desiring beer. But, of course, the question cannot be settled in such a simple way. The real difficulty … is that the extraordinary position of man in the physical universe makes it practically impossible to treat him in either one direction or the other in a purely physical way. Man is an exception, whatever else he is …

Man is always something worse or something better than an animal; and a mere argument from animal perfection never touches him at all. Thus, in sex no animal is either chivalrous or obscene. And thus no animal ever invented anything so bad as drunkenness – or so good as drink …

I believe that if by some method the local public-house could be as definite and isolated a place as the local post office or the local railway station, if all types of people passed through it for all types of refreshment, you would have the same safeguard against a man behaving in a disgusting way in a tavern that you have at present against his behaving in a disgusting way in a post office: simply the presence of his ordinary sensible neighbours. In such a place the kind of lunatic who wants to drink an unlimited number of whiskies would be treated with the same severity with which the post office authorities would treat an amiable lunatic who had an appetite for licking an unlimited number of stamps ... It is an essential matter that in both cases the authorities could rapidly communicate with the friends and family of the mentally afflicted person. At least, the postmistress would not dangle a strip of tempting sixpenny stamps before the enthusiast's eyes as he was being dragged away with his tongue out.[142]

Stephen Leacock (1869-1944)

The Canadian humorist Stephen Leacock was an academic (he was Professor of Political Economy at McGill University) and a public speaker who commanded the same kind of popularity as did Charles Dickens. He was master of the low-key, satirical, perfectly reasonable account of the vices and virtues of humanity; but nobody reading his account of the 'temperance' of Mr Rasselyer-Brown could miss the real point. This is as powerful a temperance tract as any abolitionist might have come up with, but the artless skill of Leacock's writing lies in the fact that it is not alcohol he is attacking.

Mr Rasselyer-Brown drank.
    It was not meant that he was a drunkard or that he drank too much, or anything of the sort. He drank. That was all.

There was no excess about it. Mr. Rasselyer-Brown, of course, began the day with an eye-opener – and after all, what alert man does not wish his eyes well open in the morning? He followed it usually just before breakfast with a bracer – and what wiser precaution can a business man take than to brace his breakfast? On his way to business he generally had his motor stopped at the Grand Palaver for a moment, if it was a raw day, and dropped in and took something to keep out the damp. If it was a cold day he took something to keep out the cold, and if it was one of those clear, sunny days that are so dangerous to the system he took whatever the bar-tender (a recognised health expert) suggested to tone the system up. After which he could sit down in his office and transact more business, and bigger business, in coal, charcoal, wood, pulp, pulp-wood, and wood-pulp, in two hours than any other man in the business could in a week. Naturally so. For he was braced, and propped, and toned up, and his eyes had been opened, and his brain cleared, till outside of very big business indeed few men were on a footing with him.

In fact, it was business itself which had compelled Mr. Rasselyer-Brown to drink. It is all very well for a junior clerk on twenty dollars a week to do his work on sandwiches and malted milk. In big business it is not possible ....

But – let it be repeated and carefully understood – there was no excess about Mr. Rasselyer-Brown's drinking. Indeed, whatever he might be compelled to take during the day, and at the Mausoleum Club in the evening, after his return from his club at night Mr. Rasselyer-Brown made it a fixed rule to take nothing. He might, perhaps, as he passed into the house, step into the dining-room and take a very small drink at the side-board. But this he counted as part of the return itself, and not after it. And he might, if his brain were over-fatigued, drop down later in the night in his pyjamas and dressing-gown when the house was quiet, and compose his mind with a brandy and water, or something suitable to the stillness of the hour, but this was not really a drink. Mr. Rasselyer-Brown called it a *nip*; and of course any man may need a *nip* at a time when he would scorn a drink.[143]

Although the word 'temperance' has become inextricably associated with the control of alcohol consumption, the word, of course, has a much wider meaning, and those who listed the virtues had more in mind when they included this one than merely staying sober. They meant by temperance avoidance of excess, practising self-control, and putting a curb on the instinct for self-indulgence. Plato considered temperance a mark of maturity and good citizenship, something to be achieved by self-control and reason; the Church has trusted self-control less and looked more to God for the power to be moderate.

John Evelyn (1620-1705/6)

Moderation is not just a personal matter, it is something to be practised by societies and states. History already condemns the flamboyant arrogance of the Romanian dictator Nicolae Ceausescu's palace in Bucharest, and the self-indulgent lifestyle enjoyed by the communist rulers of that impoverished country. But such intemperance is not the sole preserve of notorious dictators. It can strike nearer home. On 12 June 1684, the diarist John Evelyn reflected ruefully on the growth of modern London:

> I went to advise and give directions about the building of two streets in Berkeley Gardens, reserving the house and as much of the garden as the breadth of the house. In the meantime I could not but deplore

that sweet place (by far the most noble gardens, courts and accommodations, stately porticos, etc. any where about the town) should be so much straighten'd* and turn'd into tenements. But that magnificent pile and gardens contiguous to it, built by the late Lord Chancellor Clarendon, being all demolish'd, and design'd for Piazzas and buildings, was some excuse for my Lady Berkeley's resolution of letting out her ground also for so excessive a price as was offer'd, advancing near £1,000 per annum in mere ground-rents; to such a mad intemperance was the age come of building about a city, by far too disproportionate already to the nation; I having in my time seen it almost as large again as it was within my memory.[144]

As Evelyn's early nineteenth-century editor William Bray remarked in a footnote, 'What would Mr. Evelyn think if he saw what is now called London?'

W. B. Yeats (1865-1939)

It is not difficult to find examples of moderation in this sense, for a moderation in living arrangements brings in many themes, from self-sufficiency to the simple life with much in between. Those who preach that kind of moderation are not slow to point out the benefits, as does, for example, the Irish poet W. B. Yeats in 'The Lake Isle of Innisfree'.

I will arise now, and go to Innisfree,
And a small cabin build there, of clay and wattles
    made:
Nine bean-rows will I have there, a hive for the
    honey-bee,

* Reduced to poverty.

And live alone in the bee-loud glade.
And I shall have some peace there, for peace comes
    dropping slow,
Dropping from the veils of morning to where the
    cricket sings;
There midnight's all a glimmer, and noon a purple
    glow,
And evening full of the linnet's wings.

I will arise and go now, for always night and day
I hear lake water lapping with low sounds by the
    shore;
While I stand on the roadway, or on the pavements
    grey,
I hear it in the deep heart's core.[145]

George Gissing (1857-1903)

That kind of temperance is often a blessing of old age – for those who are blessed with prosperity and contentment in retirement. The desires and ambitions of youth slow down as we grow old. Living to a good old age and remaining in reasonable health are what most people hope for.

The Private Papers of Henry Ryecroft is an elegiac meditation by an old man who, after a life of hardship and poverty, finds himself comfortably provided for and living in rural retirement. Gissing's own life as a writer was a hard one (portrayed to some extent in his novel *New Grub Street*), and the *Private Papers* no doubt contain a fair amount of wish-fulfilment.

So, once more, the year has come full circle. And how quickly; alas, how quickly! Can it be a whole twelvemonth since the last spring? Because I am so content with life, must life slip away, as though it grudged me my happiness? Time was when a year drew its slow length of toil and anxiety and ever

168

frustrate waiting. Further away, the year of childhood seemed endless. It is familiarity with life that makes time speed more quickly. When every day is a step in the unknown, as for children, the days are long with the gathering of experience; the week gone by is already far in retrospect of things learnt, and that to come, especially if it foretell some joy, lingers in remoteness. Past mid-life, one learns little and expects little. Today is like unto yesterday, and to that which shall be the morrow. Only torment of mind or body serves to delay the indistinguishable hours. Enjoy the day, and behold, it shrinks to a moment.

I could wish for many another year; yet, if I knew that not one more awaited me, I should not grumble. When I was ill at ease in the world, it would have been hard to die; I had lived to no purpose, that I could discover, the end would have seemed abrupt and meaningless. Now, my life is rounded; it began with the natural irreflective happiness of childhood, it will close in the reasoned tranquillity of the mature mind. How many a time, after long labour on some piece of writing, brought at length to its conclusion, have I laid down the pen with a sigh of thankfulness; the work was full of faults, but I had wrought sincerely, had done what time and circumstance and my own nature permitted. Even so may it be with me in my last hour. May I look back on life as a long task duly completed – a piece of biography; faulty enough, but good as I could make it – and, with no thought but one of contentment, welcome the repose to follow when I have breathed the word 'Finis'.[146]

Malcolm Muggeridge (1903-1990)

However, such meditations are sometimes given a cynical reception, especially by those who are still young and are not inclined to be moderate yet. Malcolm Muggeridge, whose Christianity was increasingly evident as he spoke out more and more strongly on ethical issues in his later life, was often accused of sour grapes in old age:

> A criticism of Malcolm which is often made is that much of what he says about human existence can be disregarded as the meditations of an elderly man who is suffering an advanced from of world-weariness. This is especially so when he talks about ethical issues; a common reaction to his stand on permissiveness and pornography is that he is someone who, too old to enjoy such things any more, is now sniping petulantly at those who still can. But this argument ignores that fact that Muggeridge has been sounding that particular clarion call for many years; and that whatever his view of the transitoriness of this world's splendours may or may not be, he enjoys the world more than many of his critics do.
>
> Nevertheless, his perspective on life is necessarily influenced by the fact that he is, as he repeatedly reminds us, bound to leave it before very long.[147]

James Ball Naylor (1860-?)

However, virtue catches up with us all in the end, or so implies the American Dr James Naylor in an interesting comment on Old Testament poetry:

> King David and King Solomon
>   led merry, merry lives,
> With many, many lady friends
>   and many, many wives,
>
> But when old age crept over them,
>   with many, many qualms,
> King Solomon wrote the proverbs
>   and King David wrote the Psalms.[148]

A.A. Milne (1882-1956)

Temperance can be a miserable virtue, and its owner can make plenty of other people miserable in the process. Here is Eeyore, the ultimate depressive toy donkey, gloomily explaining to Christopher Robin and the world at large that he doesn't really need a house so the sudden disappearance of his dwelling is therefore neither here nor there (much the same might be said of his dwelling, in fact …) – but that, on the other hand, perhaps *something* might be recovered from the tragedy.

> 'Sometimes,' said Eeyore, 'when people have quite finished taking a person's house, there are one or two bits which they don't want and are rather glad for the person to take back, if you know what I mean. So I thought if we just went – '
>
> 'Come on,' said Christopher Robin, and off they hurried.[149]

John Dryden (1631-1700)

It needn't be like that. Moderation, even abstinence, can be a winsome trait. Here is Chaucer's Parson pilgrim, whom we have met before (p.17), embellished approvingly by John Dryden:

> A Parish-Priest was of the Pilgrim-Train:
> An Awful, Reverend, and Religious Man.
> His Eyes diffus'd a venerable Grace,
> And Charity it self was in his Face.
> Rich was his Soul, though his Attire was poor;
> (As God had cloth'd his own Ambassador);
> For such, on Earth, his bless'd Redeemer bore.
> Of Sixty Years he seem'd; and well might last
> To Sixty more, but that he liv'd too fast;

171

Refin'd himself to Soul, to curb the Sense;
And made almost a Sin of Abstinence.
Yet, had his Aspect nothing of severe,
But such a face as promis'd him sincere.
Nothing reserv'd or sullen was to see,
But sweet Regards; and pleasing Sanctity:
Mild was his accent, and his Action free,
With Eloquence innate his Tongue was arm'd;
Tho' harsh the Precept, yet the Preacher
    charm'd;
For, letting down the golden Chain from high,
He drew his Audience upward to the Sky ...[150]

The author of 'The Whole Duty of Man'

For over a century, three books were to be found in the
home of any English Christian who could read: the
Authorised Version of the Bible, *The Pilgrim's Progress*, and
The Whole Duty of Man.

The author, whose identity is not known (but Richard
Allestree the Oxford Professor of Divinity c.1657, is
probably the likeliest candidate), intended to produce a
compendium of the Christian life for an age that is in many
ways remarkably like our own. There were several imi-
tations, but *The Whole Duty* retained its popularity.

The book is a manual of Christian conduct; sins and
virtues are very much its focus. Yet one of the remarkable
characteristics of the book is the author's ability to portray
duty as pleasure – the pleasure of redeemed individuals
living with gratitude before Christ. For that reason there is
much reassurance and compassion in the book, and warm
recognition that men and women are only human!

The extract below (on the duty of temperance in dress)
is taken from Michael Perry's fresh and relevant rendering
of the book into modern language, emphasising its
continuing relevance.

Remember that clothes don't add any real value to a person. So it's simply not good enough to spend a major part of your time thinking about, or spending a lot of your money on, them. You shouldn't value yourself more because of what you are able to afford, or despise others who can't afford to dress well. When you are choosing what you are going to wear, remember St. Peter's advice to the women of his time:

> Your beauty should not come from outward adornment, such as braided hair and the wearing of gold jewellery and fine clothes. Instead it should be that your inner self, the unfading beauty of a gentle and quiet spirit, which is of great worth in God's sight. (1 Peter 3:3,4)

Dress yourself with real Christian goodness – that's the clothing which will make you attractive in God's eyes – and to the eyes of other people too. For unless your onlookers are idiots they will value you more for being good than for being ostentatious. And one ordinary coat you give to a poor friend will make you look much better than twenty plush coats you put on your own back.

Although I've talked of moderation in detail, I want to add this warning. I have been highlighting the fault of *excess*, yet it's quite possible to fall into the opposite error – of being so miserly or careless of health and limb that you don't look after yourself properly. There are those who are so busy in their jobs that they deprive themselves of the adequate sleep and the recreation that they really need. In other words, don't read what I have said so far and pat yourself on the back because of your self-restraint, when you are so busy getting money that you haven't got time to eat!

The love of money is a source of all kinds of evil. Some have been so eager to have it that they have wandered away from the faith and have broken their hearts with many sorrows. (1 Timothy 6:10).[151]

Conclusion

The seven deadly sins and the seven virtues have stirred up strong emotions over the centuries, and provoked many sermons and many rebukes. Today they are almost a joke, and few take them seriously. If we say of somebody that 'She is a virtuous lady', it seems quaint and often rather old-fashioned. On the other hand, 'He's an old reprobate', or 'The old sinner!' can often sound almost endearing.

Why has this happened?

The tendency of character to become stereotyped

We have seen many examples of the debasing of virtues in this book. Fortitude, for example, can become a kind of gung-ho bravery that ends up as self-seeking and no virtue at all. Here for example is the back-cover blurb of a 1961 book that reflects male chauvenism *par excellence*.

> *The Man's Book:* This exciting, entertaining, big-value omnibus series for men ... Action, suspense and thrills are the essential qualities of all the stories which are selected, from the pick of *all* the publishers' lists, by an all-male editorial board who *know* the kind of tough, hard-hitting reading that men prefer ... vigorous, virile reading of high quality, in fine bindings at low cost....[152]

Talbot Baines Reed and Dean Farrar had a point: often real male virtues come in unexpected guises. Sometimes what gains popular approval is more a sin of complacency than a virtue of fortitude. Thus the ancient concept of deadly sins and moral virtues becomes irrelevant – at least, so far as contemporary popular heroes are concerned.

The relative world in which we live

The modern world is different to that of earlier centuries. It has largely dispensed with the belief that an absolute source for virtue or an absolute yardstick for sin exist. In our 'post-modernist' age, good and evil are largely relative. How you act depends on what the situation is at the time. We don't speak about the seven deadly sins and the seven virtues very much nowadays, because we don't look at sin and virtue in the same way that people once did.

Of course, sins and virtues have not disappeared, despite the fact that pundits often write off modern society as selfish and self-seeking. But that ignores the virtues we often practise *as* a society; corporate compassion in the face of global tragedy, for example, as the relief trucks trundle to the latest famine, flood or earthquake, and people who don't have a lot themselves give what they can ill afford, because they want to help.

Many, perhaps most, see sin and virtue like that: in terms of their consequences for others. It's a good point; whatever label we give to our society, it *is* a society, and it is other people whom our sins and virtues affect. In compiling this anthology I have been struck by how often sin and virtue are seen not so much in the way they corrupt or enhance the person practising them, but the effect they have on the people who witness them.

The problem with relative morality is that it can be hard to find a way of making any effective moral judgements at all. In every age, saints and sinners are often hard to recognise. Some-times, it's difficult to tell them apart; more so than ever, perhaps, today.

Here is one of the truly great – and truly human – beings of the second world war:

> Don't thank me for your survival. Thank your people who worked day and night to save you from extermination .... In the end I request you all to keep a three minute silence, in memory of the countless victims among you who have died in these cruel years.[153]

Oskar Schindler, who saved thousands of Jews from death and was declared a Righteous Person by the Israeli people after the war, was still a human being. After the war, his life was a catalogue of personal failings, as Thomas Kenneally describes in his moving tribute *Schindler's Ark*.[154]

Was Oskar Schindler a virtuous man? It depends on who you ask. Was he a sinful man? It depends on who you ask.

The spiritual dimension

It was theologians who first discussed the seven deadly sins and the seven virtues, and they remain the experts in the field. All the great world religions condemn sin and extol virtue. 'Make me virtuous, Lord, but not yet,' prayed St Augustine, proving that even the greatest theologians have to grapple with the basics.

With the decline of religion as a factor in everyday Western life, interest in an absolute concept of sin and of virtue has declined too. It's a loss that has been recognised by many observers, of all faiths and none. Previous generations were able to measure their conduct against an absolute yardstick of sins and virtues. In our Generation X society, that accepted yardstick has gone. A symbolic moment recounted by Douglas Coupland speaks for a generation:

> While Daisy and Mark stood by the candles, I fetched a box of decorative matches from the fireplace, returned to the table, and relit the candles. Once these candles were all burning fully, the three of us moved in on them, and without speaking, we blew them out together, just as Jasmine was walking back in the door.
>
> 'What are you kids doing?' she asked us, but we never replied, and we walked into the kitchen, The moment was not one that could be talked about. The moment was entirely ours. As brothers and sister we knew

177

instinctively that if we were going to stand in darkness, best we stand in a darkness we had made ourselves.[155]

Darkness as a metaphor for a spiritual void is not new: Joseph Conrad used it long ago:

> Marlow ceased, and sat apart, indistinct and silent, in the pose of a meditating Buddha. Nobody moved for a time. 'We have lost the first of the ebb,' said the Director, suddenly. I raised my head. The offing was barred by a black band of clouds, and the tranquil waterway leading to the uttermost ends of the earth flowed sombre under an overcast sky – seemed to lead into the heart of an immense darkness.[156]

The message of religion, however, is that the darkest hour comes before the dawn. The sun was eclipsed when Jesus was crucified, but Easter followed. In Anthony Burgess's epic novel *Earthly Powers* (1980), it is at the novel's dark centre point that a light lances the darkness in the shape of simple acts of charity and compassion in a Malaysian hospital. As Abigail Adams wrote to her husband, John Quincy Adams, the second president of the American republic:

> It is not in the still calm of life, or the repose of a pacific station, that great characters are formed ... Great necessities call out great virtues. [157]

Religion and the virtues and sins that proceed from it, despite many reports to the contrary, are not dead; the sins and virtues are as much part of today's world as they were of the world of the Desert Fathers, who first named them centuries ago.

SOURCES

1. Bernard Shaw, *Major Barbara* (1907), final scene.

2. Genesis 4:7 (Authorised Version of the Bible).

3. Augustine, *Confessions* (c.AD 398), 8.xi. For more examples of the seven deadly sins in the Church Fathers and in medieval allegory, see e.g. C.S. Lewis, *The Allegory of Love* (Oxford University Press, 1936), chapter 2.

4. Thomas Merton, a twentieth-century monk, gives a useful introduction in the book cited below.

5. Thomas Merton, *The Wisdom of the Desert* (Sheldon Press, 1961), p.19.

6. Thomas Dekker, *The Seven Deadly Sins of London* (1606).

7. Geoffrey Chaucer, *The Canterbury Tales, The Parson's Tale, part 3* (c.1400).

8. William Langland, *Piers the Ploughman* (1550), my translation, Passus 5.

9. 1 Samuel 18:6-9 (New International Version of the Bible).

10. Dante, *Divine Comedy* (1472), Purgatorio Cantos x-xii.

11. The letter and its circumstances can be found in Ernest Newman, *Wagner as Man and Artist* (John Lane, the Bodley Head, 1925), p.13.

12. Quoted in Allan M. Laing, ed., *In Praise of Bernard Shaw* (Muller, 1949), p.35.

13. Cf Peter Quennell, *Four Portraits: Studies of the 18th Century* (Collins, 1945), p.34.

14. Oscar Wilde, 'Phrases and Philosophies for the Use of the Young' (1894).

15. Hesketh Pearson, *The Life of Oscar Wilde* (1946), pp.58-59.

16. Logan Pearsall Smith, ed., *Donne's Sermons: Selected Passages* (Oxford University Press, 1919), pp.180-182.

17. Grahame's biographer Peter Green is quite sure of this and points out that the trial of Toad in *The Wind in the Willows* is a transmutation into fantasy of Wilde's trial twelve years earlier. See Peter Green, *Kenneth Grahame: a Biography* (John Murray, 1959), p.166.

18. Kenneth Grahame, *The Wind in the Willows* (Methuen, 1908; new edn 1981), pp.226-227.

19. William Langland, *ibid.*

20. Robert Browning, 'Soliloquy of the Spanish Cloister', *Dramatic Lyrics* (1842).

21. Lewis Carroll, *Through the Looking-Glass: and What Alice Found There* (1872), chapter 4.

22. Ephesians 4:26 (New International Version of the Bible).

23. Jonathan Swift, letter to Alexander Pope, 26 November 1725. Quoted in Bonamy Dobrée, *English Literature in the Early Eighteenth Century 1700-1740* (Oxford [History of English Literature vol. vii], 1959, p.447.

24. Jonathan Swift, *A Modest Proposal* (1727) in John Hayward, *Swift: Gulliver's Travels and Selected Writings in Prose and Verse* (Nonesuch Press, 1968), p.512.

25. Samuel Johnson, Letter to Lord Chesterfield, 7 February 1755.

26. G.K. Chesterton, 'Antichrist …' in *Poems* (Burns and Oates, 1915).

27. Psalm 4:4; Ephesians 4:26 (New International Version of the Bible).

28. Larry Crabb, *Inside Out* (Navpress, 1988), pp. 67-68.

29. Jonathan Edwards, *Dissertation Concerning the Nature of True Virtue* (1788), chapter iv.

30. William Blake, 'A Poison Tree' in *Songs of Experience* (1794).

31. William Blake, 'Auguries of Innocence' (c.1803).

32. William Blake, 'Proverbs of Hell', *The Marriage of Heaven and Hell* (1790-93).

33. *Ibid.*

34. William Blake, 'The French Revolution' (1791).

35. William Blake, 'Jerusalem' (1804-1820).

36. William Blake, 'The Everlasting Gospel' (c.1818).

37. Isaac Watts, Song XVII, *Divine Songs* (1715).

38. William Langland, *ibid.*

39. Philippians 4:10-13 (New International Version of the Bible).

40. Luke 15:11-31 (New International Version of the Bible).

41. Enid Blyton, *Go Ahead, Secret Seven!* (Brockhampton Press, 1953), pp.10-12.

42. William Shakespeare, *The Merchant of Venice* (1596), Act 3 scene ii.

43. William Shakespeare, *Othello* (1604), Act 3 scene iii.

44. *Ibid.*

45. Exodus 20:1-6 (New International Version of the Bible).

46. Deuteronomy 32: 6-29 (New International Version of the Bible).

47. William Langland, *ibid.*

48. C.S. Lewis, *The Pilgrim's Regress* (Geoffrey Bles, New revised edn 1943), p.30.

49. Robert Alley, *Last Tango in Paris* (1973), p.41.

50. T.H. White, *The Ill-Made Knight*, part 3 of *The Once and Future King* (Collins, 1958), p.348.

51. William Shakespeare, 'The Rape of Lucrece' (1594), verses 31, 72, 99.

52. William Shakespeare, Sonnet 129.

53. George Bernard Shaw, *Man and Superman*, Act III (Constable, 1927), p. 121.

54. 'The Form of the Solemnization of Matrimony', *Book of Common Prayer* (1662).

55. Dorothy L. Sayers, *The Other Six Deadly Sins* (Methuen, 1943), pp.4-5.

56. William Langland, *ibid.*

57. Kenneth Grahame, *The Wind in the Willows* (Methuen, 1908; new edition 1981), p.16.

58. *Ibid.*, p.38.

59. Robert Farrar Capon, *The Supper of the Lamb* (Doubleday 1969), p.109.

60. Laurie Lee, 'Appetite', in *I Can't Stay for Long* (Penguin, 1977), p.64.

61. Frank Richards, *Billy Bunter of Greyfriars School* (Armada edition, 1968), p.192.

62. Robert Backhouse, ed., *The Spiritual Exercises of St Ignatius of Loyola* (Hodder and Stoughton, 1989), p.52.

63. Desmond Tutu, quoted in Naomi Tutu, *The Words of Desmond Tutu* (Hodder Spire, 1989), p.37.

64. Table based on statistics from Christian aid, and printed in: Kathy Keay, *How to Make the World Less Hungry* (IVP Frameworks, 1990), p.78.

65. R. L. Stevenson, 'Happy Thought' in *A Child's Garden of Verses* (1885).

66. Aldous Huxley, *Brave New World* (1932), chapter 3.

67. Vance Packard, *The Waste Makers* (Penguin, 1963), pp.47-48.

68. Amos 5:1,11-24 (New International Version of the Bible).

69. William Langland, op. cit., p.67.

70. St Augustine, *Confessions* (c.398), 2.vi.

71. Mark Twain, *Pudd'nhead Wilson* (1894), chapter 2.

72. George MacDonald, *What's Mine's Mine* (1886), chapter xxxii, quoted in: Rolland Heim, ed., *The World of George MacDonald: Selections From His Works of Fiction* (Harold Shaw, 1978), p.107.

73. Dorothy L. Sayers, *The Other Six Deadly Sins* (Methuen, 1943), p.16.

74. William Langland, *ibid.*

75. Jerome K. Jerome, *The Idle Thoughts of an Idle Fellow* ... (Field and Tuer, 1889), p.45.

76. Dorothy L. Sayers, *op. cit.*, p.24

77. Talbot Baines Reed, *Parkhurst Boys* (Boys's Own Paper, undated but after 1891), pp.220-222.

78. Geoffrey Hill, *Tenebrae* (Andre Deutsch, 1978), p.21.

79. John Berryman, *Love & Fame* (Faber and Faber, 1971), p.83.

80. Isaac Watts, *Divine Songs* (1715), p.46.

81. Lewis Carroll, *Alice's Adventures in Wonderland* (1865), chapter 10.

82. *Ibid.*

83. William Law, *A Serious Call to a Devout and Holy Life: Adapted to the State and Condition of All Orders of Christians* (1729), chapter vii.

84. Proverbs 6:6-11 (New International Version of the Bible).

85. 1 Corinthians 13:1-12 (Authorised Version of the Bible).

86. M. A. Reid, 'Theological Virtues', in D. J. Atkinson and D. H. Field, eds, *New Dictionary of Christian Ethics and Pastoral Theology* (Inter-Varsity Press, 1995), p.844.

87. Walter Savage Landor, 'Around the Child'. Landor's *Complete Works* were published in 1846.

88. Jeremiah 32:6-44 (New International Version of the Bible).

89. Luke 18:16-17 (New International Version of the Bible).

90. Richard Wurmbrand, *From the Lips of* Children (Hodder and Stoughton, 1986), pp.16-17.

91. Hebrews 11:1-39 (New International Version of the Bible).

92. William Blake, 'The Marriage of Heaven and Hell' (1790-93), plates 17-20.

93. Francis A. Schaeffer, *He is There and He is Not Silent* (Hodder and Stoughton, 1972), p.95-96.

94. Julian of Norwich, *Revelations of Divine Love* (c.1373-1443), thirteenth vision.

95. Alfred Tennyson, *Poems* (1842), vol. 1.

96. H. G. Wells, 'The Time Machine', Epilogue: in *The Time Machine and Other Stories* (1895).

97. William Morris, *News From Nowhere* (1891), chapter vii.

98. Voltaire, trs Tobias Smollett, *Candide* (1759), chapter xxx.

99. Michael Coren, *Gilbert: The Man who was Chesterton* (Jonathan Cape, 1989), pp.186-187.

100. G.K. Chesterton, *The Ballad of the White Horse* (1911), Bk 1, Bk 3.

101. H. W. Longfellow, 'The Building of the Ship', in *The Oxford Dictionary of Quotations* (OUP, second edition 1953), p.316.

102. Arthur Hugh Clough, 'Say not the Struggle Naught Availeth', in Arthur Quiller-Couch, *The Oxford Book of Victorian Verse* (OUP, 1922), p.327.

103. Adrian Plass, 'Playground'. Printed in various publications, e.g. in Adrian Plass (illustrated by Ben Ecclestone), *Learning to Fly: a Shared Journey* (Solway, 1996), p.13.

104. Walter A. Raleigh, 'Laughter from a cloud' (1923).

105. Hilaire Belloc, 'The Good Woman', in *Hills and the Sea* (1906).

106. W.H. Auden, 'Twelve Songs: IX' (1936, in W.H. Auden, ed. Edward Mendelson, *Collected Poems*, Faber and Faber, 1991), p.141.

107. C.S. Lewis, *The Four Loves* (1960: Collins Fontana, 1993), p.107.

108. Mervyn Peake, *Titus Groan* (1946) in *The Gormenghast Trilogy* (Mandarin, 1992), p.63.

109. *Ibid.*, p.206.

110. *Ibid.*, p.247.

111. Sister Wendy Beckett, *Meditations on Love* (Dorling Kindersley, 1995), p.36.

112. Jack Clemo, *The Marriage of a Rebel* (Gollancz), 1980, pp.30-31.

113. Mother Teresa of Calcutta, quoted in Malcolm Muggeridge, *Something Beautiful for God* (Collins Fontana, 1972), pp.73-74.

114. Mother Teresa of Calcutta, *The Love of Christ: Spiritual Counsels* (Collins Fount, 1982), p.73.

115. Deuteronomy 7:7-15 (New International Version of the Bible).

116. George Herbert, 'Love III', in *The Temple* (1633).

117. Plato, Benjamin Jowett trs, *The Republic*, IV.443.

118. R.C. Roberts, 'Virtue, Virtues', in D. J. Atkinson and D.H. Field, eds, *New Dictionary of Christian Ethics and Pastoral Theology* (Inter-Varsity Press, 1995), p.881.

119. Anthony Trollope, *Orley Farm* (1862), chapter 8.

120. Job 31:10-31 (New International Version of the Bible).

121. Charles Dickens, *Hard Times* (1854), Book 1, chapter 2.

122. William Blake, 'The Mental Traveller', in the Pickering Manuscript, c.1805.

123. C.S. Lewis, *The Voyage of the Dawn Treader* (Geoffrey Bles, 1952: Puffin, 1965), pp.175-176.

124. Psalm 73:1-17 (New International Version of the Bible).

125. Dietrich Bonhoeffer, David McI. Gracie ed. and trs, *Meditating on the Word* (Cowley, 1986), pp.143-144.

126. 1 Kings 3:16-28 (New International Version of the Bible).

127. Mark Twain, *A Connecticut Yankee at King Arthur's Court* (1889), chapter 35: 'A Heartrending Incident'.

128. Matthew 18:21-35 (New International Version of the Bible).

129. William Shakespeare, *Measure for Measure* (1604), Act 2, scene ii.

130. Martin Luther, *The Bondage of the Will [De Servo Arbitrio, 152 5]*, J. I. Packer and O. R. Johnston trss (James Clarke, 1957), pp. 316-317.

131. Thomas Watson, 'A Preliminary Discourse to Catechising', in *A Body of Divinity* (part of *A Body of Practical Divinity*, 1692: this edition Banner of Truth, revised edition 1965), p.95.

132. Ambrose Bierce, *The Devil's Dictionary*, originally published as *The Cynic's Word Book* (1906).

133. John Cassian, *The Conferences of Cassian* (Conf. 18), in Owen Chadwick, ed. and trs, *Western Asceticism* (SCM: Library of Christian Classics XII, 1958), pp.273-274.

134. F.W. Farrar, *St Winifred's: or the World of School* (1862), chapter xvii.

135. Talbot Baines Reed, *The Fifth Form at St Dominic's* (1881), chapter xix.

136. John Bunyan, *Pilgrim's Progress Part II* (1684), final pages.

137. George Orwell, *Animal Farm: a Fairy Story* (1945), chapter vi.

138. Terry Waite, *Taken on Trust* (Hodder and Stoughton, 1993), pp.86-87

139. Robert F. Scott, quoted in Apsley Cherry-Garrard, *The Worst Journey in the World* (Penguin, 1937), vol. ii, p.529. I have abridged Barrie's extracts from the letter.

140. J. M. Barrie, *Courage* (Hodder and Stoughton, [1922]), unpaged.

141. Magnus Magnusson and Hermann Pálsson, trss, *Njal's Saga* (Penguin, 1960), pp. 267-68.

142. G.K. Chesterton, 'Wine When it is Red', in *All Things Considered* (1908).

143. Stephen Leacock, *Arcadian Adventures with the Idle Rich* (1914), chapter iv.

144. John Evelyn, *Diary* (1641-1706: Frederick Warne, William Bray ed., c. 1818), p.458.

145. W.B. Yeats, 'The Lake Isle of Innisfree', in *The Rose* (1893).

146. George Gissing, *The Private Papers of Henry Ryecroft* (Constable, 1903), pp.275-276.

147. David Porter, *A Disciple of Christ: Malcolm Muggeridge's Practical Christianity* (Marshalls, 1983), p.44.

148. James Ball Naylor, quoted in *Verse and Worse, a Private Collection by Arnold Silcock* (Faber and Faber, 1952), p.262.

149. A.A. Milne, *The House at Pooh Corner* (1928), chapter 1.

150. John Dryden, *The Character of a Good Parson: Imitated from Chaucer and Inlarg'd* (1700).

151. Michael Perry, ed., *The Whole Duty of Man: in Today's English* (Ark Publishing, 1980), pp.74-75.

152. *The Man's Book*, omnibus of novels by Al Morgan, Walter S. Tevis and Michael Cronin (Odhams, 1961), dust jacket flap.

153. Thomas Keneally, *Schindler's Ark* (Hodder and Stoughton, 1982), p.374.

154. See note above.

155. Douglas Coupland, *Shampoo Planet* (Touchstone, 1993), pp.80-81.

156. Joseph Conrad, the closing lines of *Heart of Darkness* (1902).

157. Abigail Adams, Letter to John Quincy Adams, 1780.

Acknowledgements

The author and publishers wish to thank the following for permission to reproduce material in this book. Biblical material, unless otherwise indicated, is taken from the New International Version of the Bible, © 1973, 1978, 1984 by International Bible Society, published in the UK by Hodder & Stoughton and in the United States by Zondervan.

Robert Farrar Capon, for *The Supper of the Lamb*; Dorling Kindersley, for *Meditations on Love* by Sister Wendy Beckett; Ruth Clemo, for *The Marriage of a Rebel* by Jack Clemo; Faber & Faber, for *Love & Fame* by John Berryman; HarperCollins, for *The Pilgrim's Regress* and *The Voyage of the Dawn Treader* by C.S. Lewis, *Something Beautiful for God* by Malcolm Muggeridge, and *The Ill-Made Knight* by T.H. White; Hodder and Stoughton, for *Go Ahead Secret Seven!* by Enid Blyton and *Taken on Trust* by Terry Waite; IVP, for *He is There and He is Not Silent* by Francis Schaeffer, and articles from *The New Dictionary of Christian and Pastoral Theology*; Methuen, for *The Wind in the Willows* by Kenneth Grahame; Norman Nibloe and Navpress, for *Inside Out* by Larry Crabb; Penguin UK, for *Tenebrae* by Geoffrey Hill, *Njal's Saga*, translated by Magnus Magnusson and Herman Palsson, and *Animal Farm* by George Orwell; Adrian Plass, for 'Playground' from *Learning to Fly*; Random House, for *Brave New World* by Aldous Huxley; Reed Books, for *The House at Pooh Corner*; SPCK, for *Confessions* by Augustine and *The Wisdom of the Desert* by Thomas Merton.

Index of Authors Quoted

191